Interesting Times?

Socialist History 24

Rivers Oram Press
London, Sydney and Chicago

Editorial Enquiries: Kevin Morgan, Department of Government, University of Manchester M13 9PL or kevin.morgan@man.ac.uk.

Reviews Enquiries: John Callaghan, School of Humanities, Languages and Social Sciences, University of Wolverhampton, Wulfruna Street, Wolverhampton WV1 1PB or j.callaghan@wlv.ac.uk

Socialist History 24 was edited by Julie Johnson, Kevin Morgan, Andy Croft, John Callaghan, Stephen Woodhams

Published in 2003
by Rivers Oram Press, an imprint of Rivers Oram Publishers Ltd
144 Hemingford Road, London, N1 1DE

Distributed in the USA by
Independent Publishers Group, Franklin Street, Chicago, IL 60610
Distributed in Australia and New Zealand by
UNIReps, University of New South Wales, Sydney, NSW 2052

Set in Garamond by NJ Design
and printed in Great Britain by T.J. International Ltd, Padstow

British Library Cataloguing in Publication Data
A catalogue record for this publication is available from the British Library
ISBN 1 85489 156 1 (hb)
ISBN 1 85489 157 X (pb)
ISSN 0969 4331

Contents

Books to be remembered (7)

T. E. B. Howarth, *Cambridge Between Two Wars* (John Saville)

John Saville, *Memoirs From The Left* (Chris Wrigley)

Paul Preston, *Doves of War: Four Women of Spain* (Tom Buchanan)

Archie Potts, *Zilliacus: A Life for Peace and Socialism* (Mark Phythian)

K. D. M. Snell and Paul Ell, *Rival Jerusalems: The Geography of Victorian Religion* (Madge Dresser)

John McIlroy, Kevin Morgan, Alan Campbell (eds), *Party People, Communist Lives: Explorations in Biography* (Matthew Worley)

Julie V. Gottlieb, *Feminine Fascism: Women in Britain's Fascist Movement, 1923–1945* (Christine Bolt)

Duncan Tanner, Chris Williams and Deian Hopkin (eds), *The Labour Party in Wales, 1900–2000* (Martin Johnes)

Jonathan Rose, *The Intellectual Life of the British Working Classes* (Jon Lawrence)

Sue Branford and Bernardo Kucinski, *Politics Transformed: Lula and the Workers' Party in Brazil* (Antoni Kapcia)

David Coates (ed.), *Paving the Third Way. The Critique of Parliamentary Socialism*; Michael Newman, *Ralph Miliband and the Politics of the New Left* (John Callow)

Notes on Contributors

John Callaghan is professor of Politics at the University of Wolverhampton and reviews editor of *Socialist History*. His recent publications include *Cold War, Crisis and Conflict. The CPGB 1951–68* (2003) and *The Retreat of Social Democracy* (2000).

Eric Hobsbawm is the author of numerous books including *The Age of Revolution*, *The Age of Capital*, *The Age of Empire* and *The Age of Extremes*. His autobiography *Interesting Times* was published in 2002. He is an editorial adviser to *Socialist History*.

David Howell is professor of Politics at the University of York and edits the *Dictionary of Labour Biography*. His latest book *MacDonald's Party* was published in 2002.

Ann Hughes is professor of Early Modern History at Keele University. Her most recent book is *The Causes of the English Civil War* (Palgrave, 2nd edn, 1998). She worked with Christopher Hill at the Open University between 1978 and 1980.

David Renton has written widely on Marxism and the politics of the far right. His recent books include *The Communist Party of Great Britain since 1920* (with James Eaden, 2002) and *Fascism, Anti-Fascism and Britain in the 1940s* (2000).

Martin Willis is a member of the Socialist History Society.

Editorial

Reminders of the links between communism and the universities in 1930s Britain are not confined to specialist publications. On the one hand, this was a period when communism attracted some of Britain's most distinguished intellectuals and intellectuals in the making. It was a decade of clear-cut commitments, symbolised by the war in Spain which, as Eric Hobsbawm wrote nearly sixty years later, seemed 'the only political cause which, even in retrospect, appears as compelling as it did in 1936'. On the other hand, this was also the decade of the Gulag and the show trials, and communism is just as likely to be associated with credulity with regard to Stalinist Russia, and with the perennial fascination of the Cambridge spy ring. In a decade increasingly dominated by war and its moral equivalents, the compulsion to take sides was strong. As with all wars, only afterwards did the costs of a suspension of disbelief in one's own side become fully apparent.

Reminders of these interconnections are ever present. Regularly, the obituary pages seem to remind us that the generation of the 1930s is slowly passing away, recently including valued members of this Society such as Brian Simon, Roger Simon and Betty Matthews. Christopher Hill's death earlier this year received particular publicity with his supposed 'exposure' as an agent of influence. Given the wars that Britain seems to be getting into the habit of fighting, the last thing needed now is a Kiplingesque belief in our country right or wrong (or left), and Martin Willis provides some salutary reflections on this rather squalid affair. At the same time, Ann Hughes provides a more fitting reminder of the work for which Hill will properly be remembered, as a historian.

Others, fortunately, are still very much with us, and we have taken the theme for this issue from the title of the recently published memoirs of one of them, Eric Hobsbawm. In a wide-ranging interview with David Howell, Hobsbawm offers some further reflection on his Cambridge years, which is supplemented by an extended feature in which a number of his Cambridge contemporaries recollect their own individual roads to communism. Also included is a 'review of the reviews' of *Interesting Times* by John Callaghan, while for his book to be remembered John Saville discusses T. E. B. Howarth's study of interwar Cambridge.

John Saville was a student communist of the 1930s, at the LSE, and has also published an autobiography, *Memoirs from the Left*, which is reviewed here by Chris Wrigley. The theme is continued in other reviews, and from the Spanish 'doves of war' discussed by Paul Preston, to Konni Zilliacus, Ralph Miliband and collective depictions of British communists and fascists, lives that were shaped by political choices made in this age of extremes are reconsidered.

Everything we know about the Cambridge communists of the 1930s, including the recollections presented here, suggests that Paul Lafargue's *The Right to be Lazy* did not figure prominently on their reading lists. Indeed, as David Renton shows in his illuminating re-evaluation of this work, both Lafargue and this book in particular have been somewhat neglected in accounts of Second International Marxism. However, David Renton makes a strong case that, in a world in which we seem incapable of using the technologies now available to us to enhance our lives, Lafargue's utopian vision remains as relevant as ever. To turn something of that vision into reality, however, brings us a lot closer to the Cambridge communists than might at first appear. Just as Auden in his poem 'Spain' cast the right to be lazy in the future, with 'the struggle' accomplished, Renton concludes his article with the reminder: So much still needs to be done.

Socialist History Titles

Requests for back issues to ro@riversoram.demon.co.uk

Previous issues of *Socialist History* include:

Eric Hobsbawm's Interesting Times

An interview with David Howell

Could we begin by talking about the first hundred pages of your autobiography? You describe growing up in Vienna and Berlin, an incredibly moving portrait of a world that has basically vanished. How did that experience shape you? How does it give a particular distinctive edge to your work as a historian?

Well, it's quite true: it has gone. Little bits of it survived in the older generation, the older emigrant generation, in New York and London; but otherwise it's just not there any more: nothing is there any more. How did it form me? In the nature of things, it had to. If you grew up in central Europe between the wars, particularly between 1918 and the rise of Hitler, you lived in a world which—well, you lived in an interim. You knew that the old world had gone. You didn't know what was going to come, but you knew that it would have to be different. I think that's one of the reasons why a lot of people looked at the Soviet Union and, as it were, read perhaps more into it than they might have done. I suppose, if I'd have been a young German or Austrian boy, I might conceivably have gone in for an ultra-right-wing nationalism, because that also stood for a total change. I must say, I could understand the feeling of these people, but of course it couldn't apply to me: partly because I was English and partly because I was Jewish. For both reasons, it didn't affect me: not my kind of gang, you see. But I think what makes it different is that people who grew up in England at the time did not have this sense of a world that had broken to pieces. All sorts of things happened to them, but they didn't really realise it had gone. Nothing that happened gave them this feeling of being on the sinking Titanic which those who lived in Germany experienced between 1931 and 1933. For us, there was no way of avoiding it.

Towards the end of the autobiography you talk about yourself as almost being an outsider in every context. You suggest that this is a strength for a historian in many ways as an inoculation against certain sorts of politics of identity that have become very prevalent.

Well, I think it's a strength, obviously. I think it's a strength because a major weakness of history is that it has been too much fixed into pre-existing frameworks: the framework of the nation state for one. So we are getting to a stage where there is a globalisation process in historiography as well as everything else, and to be able to see things as it were from outside will be necessary. It's somewhat easier to do if you've been on the edge, as I really have been. I'd agree I've been an outsider in that sense. But I've felt pretty comfortable in a lot of places, not least in Great Britain, and culturally and in my intellectual style I'm far more British than anything else. But I find it possible to see slightly outside it.

So this is part of an ability not to take the assumptions of a society for granted?

I don't know. I may well take some of them for granted. But some of the more obvious ones I don't take for granted so easily because I've been else-where.

I wonder if you looked at people who had not had these experiences, who were undeni-ably English or Scottish or Welsh, whether class for instance would make a similar difference.

Well, if they can't compare it with anything else, they are to that extent more limited.

I think that's an important point about the centrality of comparison to your work. Can we move onto England: Marylebone Grammar School; King's College, Cambridge, where you read for both parts of the History tripos. From most of your writings, not just the autobiography, it seems to me that with the exception of Postan you didn't get much from the established Cambridge historians. You said that at Cambridge at that time Marxist philosophers were mainly Wittgensteinians, economists were generally sympathetic to Keynes; there was no-one in the historical school, except for Postan, about whom you write very positively, that you could say that about.[1] Is that a fair comment?

Oh, absolutely. It's just conceivable that if I'd have been a medievalist at that time, and listened to Barraclough, who was a young medievalist, I might have got something out of him because he clearly was better than the rest.[2] But most of the people that one found at Cambridge were no good at all, and of course the basis, one could say the house-style of Cambridge modern history, was exactly what I reacted against. They told me that I had to start off by reading Acton's Lectures on Modern History for my scholarship.[3] I read that and I said that that is exactly the kind of history that is no good.

From what vantage point were you critical of the established Cambridge history? Was this because you'd already read some Marxist texts that gave you an alternative viewpoint?

No. There weren't all that many Marxist texts to read, and you wouldn't necessarily have come across them in Marylebone Grammar School or Marylebone Public Library at that time. I read Marxist historians, such as they were, when I got to Cambridge. There were a few, including unofficial ones: mostly Germans. I had tried to form my Marxist opinions when I was at school: not in Berlin, where I was too much involved in politics, but in England when I didn't have anything better to do. I read enormously. I used to go down from school in the lunch break to Covent Garden, when the CPGB had a little bookshop in King Street, with Jack Cohen, who became the student organiser, who was serving in there. I used to buy all those little books: the Little Lenin Library, and also German elementary Marxist texts. So I read the usual stuff that was then available and of course, from 1934 or 1935 I got the Marx-Engels selected correspondence, which was extraordinarily helpful.[4] Marxist works were becoming available for us to read; and I read them on my own because there was no-one to discuss them with.

How far were you aware of the tradition of radical liberal historiography within England? I'm thinking of people like the Hammonds for instance.[5]

Oh, I was very aware of that. It so happened that my history master, Llewellyn Smith, was very much in touch with that tradition. His father was the Llewellyn Smith, the man who wrote the history of the dockers' strike and a great figure: a Liberal but definitely a social Liberal.[6] He didn't know anything about Marx but he did know about this tradition and he did put me onto the Hammonds. I believe that at one time he sent some of my essays to the Webbs because his family knew the Webbs. Of course, he let me read his own books. Certainly, I knew about the Hammonds and naturally from that time on had a positive view of them.

The other reference I found, not in the autobiography but in the essay you wrote on the Communist Party Historians' Group, was that you'd read C.L.R. James's The Black Jacobins.[7] *When was that?*

That was rather later. I don't think that came out until when I was at Cambridge in 1938. That's a curious situation because Caribbean blacks were the only group who produced, first of all, a set of very distinguished intellectuals, both the French and the English-speaking ones. In England they were the only ones that produced a circle of dissident Marxist intellectuals. They were never a communist party group, so we were always somewhat uncertain about them. But on the other hand it was perfectly clear this was Marxist thinking: people like Arthur Lewis, C. L. R. James, and then later on Eric Williams. It's very remarkable, particularly if you compare them with black Americans and with later black immigrants into this country.

There is a seminal moment for James which may be very important. In 1932 he came to England because Learie Constantine became the Nelson professional cricketer, and Nelson was where the ILP had a strong branch. So there are contingencies which I think may be extremely important in the making of James.

Actually, I would say that colonials, as we used to call them, were very important. I remember that before I went to Cambridge, in my last year or two of school, there was a discussion group which was organised somewhere up in Edgware, where we lived, by an Indian called Har Dayal. That was the first time I really got to know and see volumes by utopian socialists. Har Dayal was a very interesting Indian who'd been a student in Britain before 1914 and became a revolutionary and played an important part in the Ghadr movement of Punjabi emigrants in America. Later on he became a sort of Indian philosopher.

If we reconstruct this world it is a lot richer and more varied than a lot of the conventional stereotypes suggest.

Oh yes, I tried to bring this out in my years in England, which were in a sense to some extent isolated, but they were lived in what you might call the grassroots intellectual circles.

I think it's important to see what this alternative historical culture was opposed to.

It was different. I don't think that really they were competing at all, I didn't regard them as competing. I regarded it as a very good preparation. People like my cousin, who then wrote *Freud and Marx*.[8] I remember going to visit him in his house and it was a little room full of pictures of Lenin and books. I forget what he was doing at the time, a teacher or something like that, trying to write pamphlets. Basically this was the kind of England that then went in for the Left Book Club: the range, the width. The idea that these people weren't reading is mistaken: on the contrary, a lot of them were reading widely, and discussing quite widely.

Did you develop any reading groups at Cambridge with other Marxists in specifically historical areas?

We had a faculty group, of course, which would meet from time to time, and somebody would come and read us papers, or we would read and discuss each other's papers. That would certainly be the case. How regularly, I don't recall.

What about the social background of the Cambridge communists? In much of the literature one gets a sense of a group that by origins was fairly middle-class. Raymond Williams clearly was not. Was Raymond unique, or were there other working-class communists at Cambridge at that time?

There weren't many working-class communists, no. But my feeling is that it was a mixed group. In the nature of things Cambridge contained a pretty fair number of people who'd gone through the sort of orthodox middle-class public school and the rest of it. But, as I tried to argue in my autobiography, I think the grammar-school element was probably over-represented; at least it was over-represented in the period of the Spanish Civil War. Before that I wouldn't know. Working-class members there clearly were: Ralph Russell, for instance, who published his own autobiography;[9] It's fairly clear that he wasn't working-class in the sense of his father being a railway signalman or something like that, but nevertheless he would be at that border. There were one or two others, George Barnard and his sister Dorothy Wedderburn were certainly were working-class: their mother was in domestic service and their father was a cabinet maker. There were some working-class communists, but in the nature of things you couldn't expect that many.

If I can now turn to the party, obviously you were with the KPD in the last days of the Weimar Republic.

Well, I was with this peculiar outfit, the socialist schoolboys.

But you joined the party formally in England?

In England, yes; in Cambridge.

How would you now want to reconstruct that experience? The autobiography is extremely informative, but there is a difference in style from the preceding chapters. Is that a fair comment?

It's a comment that's been made. To some extent of course it's natural because in the first part, up to the time I go to Cambridge, I'm talking about a situation or a period when virtually everybody concerned is dead except me. So you can't get into trouble. Later on this is not so. But it's also probably so that once I had a chance of plunging into politics, the personal was somehow or other less important.

If you look at the post-war period, as a party member from 1945 to 1956 this must clearly have been a period of declining hopes. I'm reminded of a comment that John Saville made to me once that the toughest time he had as a communist was during the Korean war, both politically and also in terms of his relations with colleagues in the University of Hull. Was that your experience?

Yes. I have no doubt at all that the really tough period was the Korean war—there was a war and we were supposed to be on the other side. I absolutely agree with John that that was a time when one's colleagues—certainly those at Cambridge—regarded you as, as it were, a Fifth Columnist, a potential Fifth Columnist. This was not so at Birkbeck which was cooler about these matters. You expected sooner or later that we'd all be rounded up. I remember thinking, if that happened, well at least it would give me a chance to do a lot of reading and writing. But it was very tough.

But you had the King's Fellowship throughout the Korean War?

Yes, I got it in 1949 and I kept it until 1955.

The other Cambridge figure of course who was very closely identified with the party and the university was Maurice Dobb. What was his experience then? Have you any sense of that?

Well, it's difficult to tell. Maurice, for one thing, never talked about these things at all. I think for Maurice the most difficult period had really been the inter-war period when he was quite isolated and marginalised. But after the war he had somehow or other managed to get himself into Trinity, and there he was, living opposite Sraffa, the two of them working together, and I mean, he was a tremendously loyal fellow.[10] He turned up to meetings and things like this, but I don't have the feeling that it was such a new thing for him to be completely isolated.

Were you heavily involved in the party in the routine sense, as opposed to your work as a historian?

No, I was involved in the party during my first marriage, where we lived, and naturally joined the local branch in St Pancras. After that, when I moved up to Cambridge I joined the graduate branch, which was a rather different thing. We did all sorts of things like publishing bulletins, but it wasn't really the same thing as ordinary party work. If I had any basic unit, that was the unit, you see. We also had one in London, but I don't believe I was in the London one until I moved back from my fellowship.

Were you in the Historians Group from when it was formed in 1946?

Yes, but I wasn't in on any of the preparatory stuff.

When you look back, the way in which the group was the crucible for many themes that have become more or less the mainstream in historiography is quite remarkable. How did you all see what you were doing at the time?

Well, we saw it in two ways. Obviously, there were the Marxist discussions. These grew essentially out of problems arising from Leslie Morton's *People's History of England* and then Maurice Dobb's *Studies in the Development of Capitalism*, which was theoretically more interesting.[11] And then of course there was Christopher Hill's own basic problem, which was the nature of the English revolution, which had been quite controversial.[12] This was the 1940 essay, but we discussed it particularly in the early years because of the tercentenary of the ending of the civil war in 1949. All sorts of theses and conclusions were put forward. I don't know if we all were completely satisfied with these, but they appeared in *Communist Review*. There were any number of debates and discussions on this subject. We also saw ourselves, I think from the start, as a sort of popular front; that's to say, a group that could organise and should organise a broad front of progressive historians against the reactionary ones. This came not only from the dons, but very largely from the schoolteachers who saw the kind of stuff that they were doing as party members was not different from the kind of history that other schoomasters and schoolteachers were doing. And so we quite deliberately developed the whole idea of a broad front of the progressives against an isolated group of reactionaries. This, of course, paid off in some ways in setting up *Past and Present*. And then of course we gradually began to show that we were producing scholarly work. One example was the Dona Torr Festschrift signalling that we'd been actually been doing some history, that we were not just propagandists.[13]

Dona Torr is an enigmatic figure. Some people in the group talk about her very positively. I get a sense that maybe you may not be so positive. Is that fair?

No, I wasn't very positive. I was never one of her favourites. Actually the only conflict I ever had with her was over that very important project of the early Historians' Group, namely the volumes of documents: *Labour's Turning Point*, they were the nineteenth century ones, and of course Christopher Hill and Edmund Dell on *The Good Old Cause*. It's a pity because these were really good collections of documents. The nineteenth-century ones failed completely, by the way. Well, it was over that: she was involved in this, and she wanted me to put in all the myths, you know: Featherstone massacre and stuff like that. I said, well, yes, fine, but you know that's not actually what happened. I knew her and went up to visit her. She wasn't an important element in my own formation as a Marxist historian, but quite clearly she was for a lot of other people.

The other issue, which comes out of your comment about the popular front and the Historians' Group, is linked to a chapter in the autobiography where you talk about the historical modernisers. The point that came out of that is that throughout the Cold War historians of very different political persuasions could actually come together on historiographical issues without political differences having an impact.

Yes, I think I've only recognised this much more clearly in retrospect, because at the time of course we disagreed. Nevertheless, it became increasingly clear that on matters of history there really was a difference between the old-fashioned cabinets and diplomacy approach to history, although this didn't always run side-by-side with the reactionaries, and the new history. This was important: we were part of a broad movement. It so happens that in this country there was a tie-up, and that tie-up was through the peculiar institutional importance of economic history in Britain. This was not necessarily the case in other countries. The significance of economic history can be seen in the case of Postan. He saw himself as a moderniser, and was passionately anti-communist. But he also knew—and I have this from his biographer, Zvi Razi—that these young Bolshies were on his side. I think that there were a lot of other people who felt that way. This is why *Past and Present* managed to build itself up. We were absolutely clear: we weren't going to start by quoting Stalin and all the rest of it, or Lenin. But if we published the right kind of stuff, it would be read, and was read by the sort of people who were not political. Look at somebody like John Elliot. Ultra-respectable: even in those days he wouldn't have dreamed of being a radical. But his kind of history, which was that of the Catalan revolution of the seventeenth century—well, we were talking about that sort of thing and it made some sort of sense: at least, enough to discuss.[14] By that time, of course, we knew what we were doing. We knew we didn't want to run this, we wanted people to come in. But in fact, until it was all over we didn't quite recognise how important we were, because through *Past and Present* we provided a sort of institutional frame for the younger against the older.

And of course in your autobiography you chart the rolling back of this achievement. I should add that economic history is no longer taught seriously at York.

Yes. Economic history did of course have the enormous advantage in those days of addressing a coherent problem, which essentially was the transformation of the medieval European economy into the modern industrial one. To this extent both Marxists and non-Marxists were trying to answer the same questions, though not always in the same terms.

I would like to touch very briefly on 1956. I take keenly the point about why you didn't leave, because the experiences that had led you to join distinguished you from other people. Yet it does seem from the book that after the events in 1956 your position was not really very different from those who had left.

No, it wasn't. I quite deliberately recycled myself. Mind you, the more I get asked this question, the harder it is to answer, because I keep wondering how far my answers are in fact projections back of something which wasn't so. The more one discusses this thing, the less one is certain of what actually happened. I didn't actually keep very much in the way of documentation at the time, so I don't know what I felt. I don't think it's an important issue, except obviously to one's autobiography. As you quite rightly say, if I hadn't insisted that I was still in the party and still had the ticket, nobody who'd read my stuff from the past forty or fifty years would necessarily have concluded I was.

Just one point on 1956, how much of a shock were Khrushchev's revelations at the CPSU's Twentieth Congress?

Oh, they were an appalling shock. You see, we all knew that all sorts of awful things had been happening. You couldn't avoid it; you couldn't not know it. And there is an enormous incentive, a motivation, simply not to believe too much, or at least not to think about it. Then comes a moment when the man gets up himself and says, 'Look, this is what Joe did'. The shock wasn't so much that—as far as we were concerned, or at least I was concerned—the shock was in seeing that the party refused to take any notice of it. You know, all this business of saying it was just the cult of personality. The cult of personality was patently not an explanation, whatever it was. That's what drove the historians into practically solid opposition: 'Look, you can't deal with this, that's not the way for Marxists to do it.'

Were there other people who reacted from their own positions in similar ways? I remember a party member who was a family friend. He was a member of the AEU, he was a shop steward; he stayed in the party after 1956, but he was basically a militant shop steward. The rest I suspect no longer mattered.

Yes, I think for working-class people that was the most important. For a lot of people, the point is they didn't join the party because of the Soviet Union. That is often forgotten. You might as well say, for instance, that people should have left the Communist Party in South Africa because of Stalin. It would have made no sense for them to think of it in those terms.

If I can pass onto the quartet, or the grand narrative, I think one of the most striking features of your whole historiographical achievement is your work as a pattern-maker: the tracing of patterns on a global basis. If you look at the four books, the first three fit into a very well-established narrative: The Age of Revolution, The Age of Capital, The Age of Empire. We then get on to Age of Extremes. That is a wonderful volume, but there is a sense when you read it of the pattern falling apart.

Well, in so far as in the first three volumes, the hope that perhaps there would be a major change is still implicit, and in the last one it clearly isn't. However, the pattern is the same, namely the phases of capitalist development. That gives a unity to all four. The combination of globalisation and—which is the same thing—the phases of the development of capitalism: this peculiar business of pushing forward and then reaching the crisis point, and then restructuring. I mean, this is perfectly Marxist, but not exclusively Marxist, as a framework. But probably only a Marxist would have systematically written it as a grand narrative.

I can see that in the first three volumes.

I think it's in the fourth one too. At least I intended it be.

Let me ask you a follow-up to that. If 1989 hadn't have happened, would volume four have been radically different?

It's not easy to see. There is a peculiar grey zone between the end of the Cold War and this year. I protected myself a bit: I used 1991 as my final point because that was the official end of the Soviet Union, that's why I used that instead of 1989. But it was quite clear, it seems to me, that you might quite conceivably have taken a different date for the end of this particular period. You might have taken a different date. If you have to choose a date, 1991 happens to be a convenient and fairly obvious one. If the Soviet Union had not actually collapsed I would probably have noted that it had ceased to be an alternative. Somebody once said, quite rightly I think, that if Andropov had gone on living for another ten years, the Soviet Union would still be there. It was Gorbachev who actually caused its collapse. We didn't foresee quite how easy its collapse would be.

I think there are tight limits to counter-factual history. One could also say that if Gorbachev had behaved differently, there might have been a different outcome.

It's possible. I know too little about it to be able to tell. It's quite clear that something dramatic was already wrong if they had to break off the plan in mid-stream. It is quite clear that the brittleness is something that nobody could foresee. I certainly think the wrong decision was taken. I think this is one of the very important reasons why the Chinese took a very different decision. But whether, having taken a different decision, it would actually have improved the long-term chances of the Soviet Union isn't so clear.

To go back to the three earlier books, how far in the whole of that narrative, which was written over several years of course, is the fact of the Soviet Union almost implicit?

Well, of course the Soviet Union is implicit because it was written in the period when the Soviet Union was a superpower.

How would you characterise 1917 now?

Well, I try to go into it in *Age of Extremes*. Now, I think it is a symptom of the crisis of the liberal capitalist world-system at that time. But for that, there would have been a Russian revolution, but there would certainly not have been a Bolshevik one.[15] Moreover, but for that not even Lenin would have been able to think it were possible to overthrow the whole show. And I think therefore that the long-term effect of this was to bring about the restructuring of the political economy of the capitalist system, at least for most of the twentieth century. They were scared by revolution. They became equally scared, some of them, by the potential of right-wing revolution, and therefore liberal capitalism had to break with the free market.

So the Bolshevik achievement was the necessary condition for effective social democracy.

That is exactly the point that I'm trying to make in *Age of Extremes*, which is a considerable step back from my youthful belief, but as a historian I think that's what I'm saying. Nobody writing the history of the world in the twentieth century could conceivably have overlooked Russia and the Russian revolution, it was such a central event. But its significance was not quite so clear at the time.

If we can pass onto the more parochial case of Britain and 'The forward march of Labour halted', which whether by accident or design is the one significant political intervention you made...

Absolutely by accident.[16]

I wonder if there ever was a forward march of labour?

Well, I wouldn't want to argue with you about this, but that's the way it looked in the 1970s. In fact, I think the forward march of labour was limited in most countries, in the sense that even in the most democratic societies it was very hard for the class party of labour to get more than 50 per cent of the vote. In England, where after all 70–75 per cent of people identified as workers, there was a limit to the forward march of labour.

I think there are two things: one is scope, the other is how contingent it was in Britain. If you look at every other European country before 1914, there was a sizeable social-democratic vote, more or less. In Britain, there was not until after 1918.

This raises one thought that I had while preparing *Labour's Turning Point*. If the Fabian line had been right and the Liberals had as it were gone in for a New Deal type of Liberalism, then they might have done what the Americans did, that is kept their labour movement on the Liberal side. But actually, it's fairly clear that they couldn't do this because right down at the bottom, the workers might have been prepared for it, but certainly the employers weren't.

I think the great weakness the Liberals had before the First World War was that they couldn't give working-class communities working-class representatives, quite apart from programmes.

Theoretically it would have been possible, but in fact we can see perfectly well why this didn't happen. I'm bound to say that it is harder to imagine a non-class or an all-class Liberal Party maintaining itself in England, which was so overwhelmingly proletarian in feeling, than in the United States, where the workers were always a minority, though in some places quite a strong one.

If I can pass onto the United States, in the quartet the United States is not a major actor. The chapter on the US in the autobiography I found an extremely good read. As a study of your own responses to the society I think it is very suggestive, but the analysis of the role of the United States in the twentieth-century I don't see as a centrepiece.

Well, I think if I had to do a major critique of my three volumes, it would certainly be that I underplay the United States, as so many people did. I didn't see it as the up-and-coming power. I didn't grasp, for instance, when I was writing *The Age of Capital* and *The Age of Empire*, how relatively huge the American economy already was, compared to the European. It's too late to rewrite the three books, but I think that is a self-criticism I would certainly want to make. I'm not quite so convinced by the criticism which Perry Anderson makes, particularly of the fourth volume, that I underplay the Asian theme, because the rise of Asia is a very late development indeed.[17] On the American case, the critique is correct.

Could it be argued that Sombart's question, however we interpret it—why is there no social-ism in the United States?—in some ways is the most important question of the twentieth century?[18]

Well, yes it could. What one needs to do is to understand why there is no social democracy in the United States. There were elements of social democracy in the United States but they were not as central as the idea of a welfare community was in Europe. I think there's no question about the specificity of American society and its values, which is something not quite the same as the force of nature of the American economy. It is something which I think we, or at least I, have not paid enough attention to.

I think the paradox is challenging because you could say in many ways that this was the purest capitalist society; this is the one where there were no feudal legacies at all and yet socialism is a marginal force.

But then of course it was also the one in which the gravediggers of capitalism, the industrial workers, were always a marginal group.

Your enthusiasm for Roosevelt I would agree with. If you look at America in the 1930s, the growth in trade union mobilisation with federal government assistance, and the militancy of that, compared with Britain, or compared with almost anywhere in the world, is quite remarkable.

Of course. Roosevelt knew that he was trying to save capitalism from itself. Nonetheless, I'm old enough to think that saving capitalism from itself is a second-best to socialism.

Notes

1. M. M. Postan began teaching at Cambridge in 1935 and became professor of Economic History in 1938. For a profile see *Interesting Times*, pp.282–5.
2. Geoffrey Barraclough (1908–84) was Fellow of St John's College, Cambridge from 1936 and published *Medieval Germany* (two volumes) in 1938. He worked on the Enigma project and after the war held chairs at Liverpool and Oxford universities, and also in the US. His most widely known book is *An Introduction to Contemporary History* (1964).
3. Acton's *Lectures on Modern History* were first published in 1906, edited and with an introduction by J. N. Figgis and R. V. Lawrence.
4. Dona Torr, ed., *Selected Correspondence of Marx and Engels* (1934).
5. J.L. and Barbara Hammond were the authors of *The Village Labourer* (1911), *The Town Labourer* (1917), *The Skilled Labourer* (1919) and other major works of social and industrial history. See Teresa Javrek, 'A New Liberal descent. The "Labourer" trilogy by Lawrence and Barbara Hammond', *Twentieth Century British History* (1999), 10, 4, pp.375–403.
6. Sir Hubert Llewellyn Smith (1869–1945) was the author, with Vaughan Nash, of *The Story of the Dockers' Strike* (1890). He was permanent secretary at the Board

of Trade from 1907 and chief economic adviser to the government 1919–27.

7. See Eric Hobsbawm, 'The Historians' Group of the Communist Party' in Maurice Cornforth, ed., *Rebels and Their Causes. Essays in honour of A. L. Morton* (1978), pp.21–47.

8. This was Ruben Hobsbaum who published two Left Book Club selections as Reuben Osborn: *Freud and Marx* (1937) and *The Psychology of Reaction* (1938); see also *Interesting Times*, p.90.

9. Ralph Russell, *Findings, Keepings. Life, Communism and Everything* (2001).

10. The economist Piero Sraffa (1898–1983) was made a Fellow of Trinity College, Cambridge having left Mussolini's Italy. A friend of Gramsci, Wittgenstein and Keynes, he was concerned with the critique of orthodox theories of value and distribution. In 1930 he began work on an edition of the complete works of Ricardo, published in eleven volumes 1951–73. His *Production of Commodities by Means of Commodities* (1960) gave rise to major debates.

11. A.L. Morton's *People's History of England* was published as a Left Book Club selection in 1938. Maurice Dobb's *Studies in the Development of Capitalism* was published in 1946.

12. Christopher Hill's essay on the English revolution was first published in Christopher Hill, ed., *The English Revolution 1640. Three Essays* (1940).

13. John Saville, ed., *Democracy and the Labour Movement* (1954).

14. Elliot was later Regius Professor at Oxford. Elliot's *The Revolt of the Catalans. A Study in the decline of Spain 1598–1640* was published in 1963. See also *Interesting Times*, p.231.

15. See on this Eric Hobsbawm's Isaac Deutscher Memorial Lecture, 'Can we write the history of the Russian Revolution?' in his *On History* (1997), pp.241–52.

16. The lecture was originally published in *Marxism Today* in September 1978. It was republished with a number of responses in Martin Jacques and Francis Mulhearn, eds, *The Forward March of Labour Halted?* (1981).

17. For Anderson's assessment see his 'Confronting defeat', *London Review of Books*, 17 October 2002. This followed his review of *Interesting Times*, also in *London Review of Books*, 3 October 2002.

18. Werner Sombart's classic sociological essay *Why Is There No Socialism in the United States?* was published in 1906.

Eric Hobsbawm's Communist Party Autobiography

From the 1930s to the 1960s, Communist Party members in Britain, as in other countries, were liable to be asked to complete a short party autobiography on certain occasions such as attending a party school, taking up party responsibilities or seeking employment with the party. Between 1950 and 1953, when there was a tightening of party rules concerning branch transfers and readmissions to membership, the number of members asked to compile autobiographies increased. However, there was never the same systematic disciplinary use of such biographies as can be traced in some other communist parties: for example in France, where the biographies were so common as to give rise to the neologism *bioter* and members were asked to indicate compromising associations and the position they had taken up at the time of the Nazi-Soviet Pact. In Britain the practice gradually died out after 1956.

The following is Eric Hobsbawm's autobiography from November 1952. Some of the questions are immediately obvious. The others are (3) Present party branch; (5) Present party responsibility; (6) Date of joining party; (7) age; (9) and (10) Questions regarding spouse's party membership; (11) 'Social origin including occupation of father'; (12) 'Education including special qualifications such as languages etc'; (13) employment and military service; (14) 'Give your reasons for joining the Party, including any previous contact you had with the working class movement. State whether you were previously a member of any other political party or organisation. Give details of your Trade Union membership, including any positions held. Give details of your party record…and positions held'; (15) Party education; (16) 'Have you had any political difference about Party policy, or any other disagreements with the Party, and how were these settled? Have you ever had any disciplinary action taken against you?' The final question asks for the respondent's evaluation of their political work and proposals for future work before providing the name of three party members to whom reference could be made.

The autobiography is held by the Labour Study and Archives Centre at the People's History Museum, Manchester.

1) Eric John Ernest Hobsbawm, King's College, Cambridge
2) 2 Nov 1952
3) Cambridge University Senior
4) University Lecturer & fellow. Cambridge & London Universities
5) Member National Univ. Staffs Ctee, National Historians Group Ctee.
6) 1936
7) Thirty five
8) Divorced
9) ——
10) ——
11) Petty-bourgeois. Father white-collar employee and small business.
12) Educated in Austria, Germany, England. MA, PhD Cambridge (History). Languages: German (bilingual), French pretty good, Spanish & Italian, rough for speaking, better for reading.
13) Student 1936–40. Army 1940–6: REs and Education Corps. Research 1946–7. University Lecturer 1947—at Birkbeck College, London. Since 1949 also Fellow of King's College, Cambridge.
14) I first came into contact with the movement when a schoolboy in Berlin, 1932. There I joined the Sozialistischer Schuelerbund, a near-party schoolboys' organisation. I was interested in the party partly by a cousin (now in Israel) who was then a Communist. Also, having lived in Vienna, where the only other party except the Social Democrats was slightly anti-semitic, I had been vaguely drawn towards the Socialists. I expect the combination of Berlin, just before Hitler came to power and rebelling against the family got me to think myself a 'Red'. Didn't do much except read, and work a little with Labour League of Youth until I came up to Cambridge in Sept 1936, regarding myself as communist. There I joined the Party.

   Trade Unions: Branch Secretary of Association of University Teachers, delegate to Council in past years. Was not eligible for TU membership until 1947.

   Branches: Cambridge University 1936–1940. St Pancras 1946–7. Clapham 1947–50. (Both localities have been divided & redivided, the name of my branch changing round.) Cambridge Univ. Senior 1950–. Also active in various professional groups.
15) I can't remember all the various schools and classes I have at various times attended.

16) Most people have political difference with the Party from time to time. I've argued them out, and the accepted party decisions until the line changed. How else are they to be settled? I've tried to stick to democratic centralism. No other disagreement I can think of. No disciplinary action against me.

17) Clear police record.

18) No dominant hobbies, but fairly wide cultural interests.

19) Fairly active in my student period all-round. Not too self-critical about that. Not so satisfied with work since coming out of Army, which has been miscellaneous, generally connected with professional groups or writing things, and tending to be rather cut off from the masses, and even from ordinary party work. (When in non-University branches I've tried to do ordinary basic work, but have kept off responsible work). Moderately satisfied with trade union work. On the whole, while there are bits and pieces I've done since the war with which I'm not too dissatisfied, I don't feel that I've done what I might for the Party, or that I've been advancing in my capacity to do so.

20) My sort of professional work is probably the best I can do, but I'd quite like if possible, to have more to do with factory workers. I've considered full-time work, but don't think I'm good enough at organising to take the idea seriously. My present occupation suits me at present.

21) Jack Cohen, James Klugmann, Rodney Hilton.

Looking Back in Amazement
Interesting Times and the reviewers

John Callaghan

For most of the reviewers of Eric Hobsbawm's autobiography the central paradox of his life is how such a brilliant scholar could be so politically wrong for fifty years of his life and *still* retain a residual loyalty to the source of his embarrassment—the Bolshevik revolution—which also happens to be one of the biggest disasters of the twentieth century. *Interesting Times* has been read as an *apologia pro vita sua* but also as an elaborate evasion of this question. The most hostile critics, such as David Pryce-Jones of the US *National Review*, solve the paradox by denying its existence.[1] In this view Hobsbawm was always a 'forger of ideas' in the service of tyranny and a man who continues to deny the moral and physical bankruptcy of communism even after its demise. Hobsbawm's academic work is dismissed as devoid of original research and dedicated only 'to prove the usual Marxist dogmas that capitalism leads to imperialism and war'—except when it makes light of 'the brute reality of Soviet terror', as in the Age of Extremes. Such critics make a useful starting point. Hobsbawm enrages them by his continued refusal to apologise for his lifelong commitment to Communism. Michael Ignatieff, Jeremy Paxman, Sue Lawley (!) and many others have tried to extract the desired confession of guilt and failed. Yet, according to his critics, Hobsbawm is feted and honoured instead of being anathematised along with the apologists of Hitler.

The faith that sustained Hobsbawm's political commitment has been boiled down to the proposition that the communist utopia was worth the sacrifice of millions of lives. Martin Amis's *Koba The Dread*, a work which appeared at the same time as *Interesting Times*, is a sustained revolt against this notion which, he says, Hobsbawm 'disgracefully' affirmed on the BBC radio programme *Desert Island Discs*.[2] Hobsbawm has indeed admitted communists believed in the justification for enormous sacrifices—'millions of lives'—when 'the shining future' was being constructed in the 1930s.[3] *Interesting Times* provides some clues as to how this could be; but in a different way so does

Koba the Dread. Amis is no historian (and it shows) but his ruminations on the Soviet catastrophe suggest, *inter alia*: that though the confessions of the Old Bolsheviks in the Moscow Trials were 'self-evidently ridiculous...yet the world, on the whole, took the other view'; that a 'reasonable excuse' for believing Stalinist propaganda was that the truth 'was entirely unbelievable'— that is 'unbelievably terrible', such was the degree of horror, cruelty, and irrationality that it entailed. Amis also suggests—a point of relevance in explaining the gulf between Soviet reality and what could be imagined by outsiders—that there is a sense that 'deep down, Russia ha[d] nothing in common with the West' (pp.7, 9, 60). To an extent, the creed apparently linking communists concealed a deeper division, because it was infused with an indigenous nihilism on the Russian side, 'at once childish and nightmarish' yet supplying 'the emotional dynamic that eventually went to make the Russian Revolution' (p.27).

Amis also lists among the elements of the Bolshevik state's strengths 'its capacity to astonish, to dumbfound—and thus to delude'. There is nothing systematic about these observations. On the contrary, they are scattered throughout the book, and it is obvious that Amis cannot see their use in answering some of his own questions. Yet he presents us with the naivety of Lenin in October 1917, imagining that socialism could be built in six months and Russia transformed in the process into 'the mightiest of states' (p.28); the widespread perception, enduring until the 1970s, of the USSR as 'fundamentally progressive' (p.39); 'the very size of Russia' for so long an aid in hiding the truth (pp.75, 93); the shared Enlightenment ideals which generated so much of the world's sympathy for the Bolshevik revolution (p.85); Russia's 'terror-famine' of 1933 coinciding, the better for its concealment and failure to register in Western minds, with the conspicuous march of the anti-Enlightenment in capitalist Europe (p.141); the fact that Stalin 'was an extremely popular leader' in the USSR 'throughout the quarter-century of his rule' (p.212); and finally, the element of self-delusion in the revolution's supporters, their faith in the Just City that could not be discarded 'without lifelong feelings of disappointment and loss' (p.273).

This is by no means an exhaustive list of the reasons why millions of people put their trust in communism. In fact, the starting point of any analysis should surely be the period when anti-capitalist parties established themselves all over Europe, when the Bolsheviks themselves were known to very few foreigners. Amis passes over all of this in silence. Most of the critics agree that Hobsbawm was indeed born into 'interesting times', but the intended irony applies just as well to the generation which preceded him. Twenty-nine million of them were either killed or wounded in the First

World War. We don't know how many people were uprooted and displaced by industrialisation, nationalism, political and economic disorder, lawlessness and the redrawing of boundaries in the years before the Bolsheviks made their presence felt. We do know that many people were convinced from their own experience that capitalism bred misery and oppression. Democracy had shallow roots in some countries, none at all in most parts of Europe. The fascist experiment in Italy, for example, was widely approved by foreigners. Parliamentary governments established after the war were soon engulfed by intractable social and economic problems which seemed to demand authoritarian solutions—mostly supplied by the political right. There was no shortage of empirical evidence for those who believed that liberal-democratic capitalism had no future (as well as no past) in most parts of the continent—including two world wars, the persecution of ethnic minorities, a global economic crisis, and the rise of fascism and dictatorship. When did it become apparent that the old Marxist choice of socialism or barbarism was false ? The advent of nuclear warfare was not such a moment, nor perhaps its later refinement with the invention of the H-bomb, widely described at the time as a weapon of genocide.

Most of the critics are agreed that the first part of *Interesting Times*, dealing with the years up to Hobsbawm's admission to Cambridge, is brilliantly evocative and revealing. Perry Anderson identifies this as one of three quite distinct parts of the book and says that it 'has many claims to be the finest piece of writing this famously accomplished stylist has ever produced'.[4] The exploration of self ends, however, when Hobsbawm deals with the period of his life when he belonged to the Communist Party. The change in register, producing for Anderson 'a sensation of discomfort…as if another sort of reader is starting to hover in the background of the narrative', signals the end of Hobsbawm's interest in his personal emotional and intellectual development. Even his own political ideas slip from view; 'The persistent pronoun is now the anonymous, generational "we".' In the chapters dealing with what it meant to be a communist Anderson points to an emphasis 'on an ethos of selfless obedience and practicality', a 'business efficiency', in Hobsbawm's own phrase, which meant that 'the appeal of the Party was that it got things done when others did not'. Anderson finds this a 'strangely lopsided' historical picture and suggests that the counterposition of barricades and theory to business efficiency is simply an *ex post facto* rhetoric which at best tells us something about the self-image of the Stalinised European Comintern, post-1926, but at worst is just another form of romanticism. Romanticised it may be, but most of Hobsbawm's party life was of course post-Comintern and in my view Anderson simply reveals his own ignorance of the appeal and mentality of the CPGB in these dismissive comments. Organisation, routine, discipline and efficiency were certainly central to the ethos of the party in the years when Hobsbawm was a member.

Anderson is right to note the absence of 'any too meticulous chronology in the discussion of [Hobsbawm's] own Communism'. Hobsbawm's reflections on the communist experience are 'insistently collective' and of his personal views 'we learn little'. His personal reaction to the milestones of Stalinism from the Moscow Trials onwards never comes to light, nor do we know what he thought about the growing literature surrounding such events, much of it written by former communists. If Hobsbawm was as shocked as other members of the party by the Khrushchev speech in 1956, it suggests that he doubted up until then what was widely believed beyond the communist membership. But we never find out what the personal shock consisted of. The suppression of self from Hobsbawm's account of his party years will be familiar, of course, to anyone who has read communist autobiographies. But we do discover the reasons for his continued membership of the party after 1956 and Anderson finds the first of these—an admission that his personal background made the break with the Party more difficult—'the plain biographical truth, well stated'. Hobsbawm's emotional attachment to the party was, then, more powerful than the dismay occasioned by 1956. Khrushchev in any case was supposed to have embarked upon de-Stalinisation and Anderson reminds us of the hope that the revolution would yet be redeemed by such efforts. Hobsbawm himself, however, tells us nothing of what he still thought possible in the Soviet Union. Yet it is clear from the historical record that many socialists continued to give the Russians the benefit of the doubt, even beyond the ranks of the communist parties. Nye Bevan is case in point. Go back to 1960 and you find many conservatives (including presidential candidates and prime ministers) who thought that the Soviet economy was yet set to surpass the West. For anyone who believed, as most Marxists did, that material progress would make social and political advances possible in the Soviet Union, there was life in the Soviet experiment yet.

It is clear to Anderson that 'at the heart of *Interesting Times* is a sustained effort to explain the meaning of a Communist life'. But it is not clear who Hobsbawm is explaining himself to. Anderson, noting Hobsbawm's recent social elevation, suggests that the unspoken addressee is an 'established order' for whom the failure of the October Revolution was self-evidently inscribed in its origins—hence Hobsbawm's neglect of close political discussion and intellectual engagement 'with the issues that haunted the trajectory of European Communism'; for this audience there is nothing to explain. There is a divided self here, though Anderson doesn't call it such. Hobsbawm, the Companion of Honour, the saviour of the Labour Party, respected academic and best-selling writer, public intellectual and friend of the great and good. But if Anderson is right, much of Hobsbawm's intended audience is unimpressed. Niall Ferguson, who wonders whether there was such a great moral difference between communism and fascism as Hobsbawm insists, concludes that the only way to understand 'this extraordinary *trahison d'un clerc*...is precisely as a succession of acts of quasi-religious faith'.[5] But for him, it was 'a curiously flexible' faith which allowed Hobsbawm to favour insurrection, in countries where he thought it was realistically on the agenda, and oppose global neo-liberalism while enjoying 'all the imaginable benefits which free capitalist democracies have to offer'. This affluent and comfortable man evidently stormed his own personal Winter Palace but, says Ferguson, continues to sympathise with a movement and creed which 'was the negation of both freedom and justice, for the sake of a spurious and ultimately bogus egalitarianism'.

Yet others find little difficulty in following the nature of Hobsbawm's commitment. He has often enough referred to the paradox of the Cold War in binding communists together against the outside world.[6] He has honestly owned up to the fact that in the 1930s, in the context of the breakdown of western capitalism, he was one of those socialists who believed that the 'brutal' experiment in Soviet Russia was worth supporting. It is not difficult to believe him when he says that 'the sheer extent of the massacres' was something they knew nothing about. It obviously discomforts many people when he reminds them that the conventional view justifies the 90 million killed or displaced in the Second World War. Yes, speaking of the Bolshevik revolution, 'in retrospect the project was doomed to failure' but, as he says, 'it took a long time to realise this': 1956 was already late in the day. Peter Preston, generally sympathetic up to this juncture, argues that Hobsbawm's 'instincts and loyalties...had become tribal' at this point.[7] His decision to remain in the party involved him in 'recycling himself', according to Neal Ascherson, a friend and former student of Hobsbawm's, 'from militant to fellow traveller' at a time when, as Ben Pimlott acknowledges, 'it was deeply unfashionable and limiting' to remain any sort of Communist.[8] The decision to stay appears to have been a mixture of hope for future de-Stalinisation and the strong pull of his 'society of great friends'. After 1968, however, as Hobsbawm has said, 'we criticised Moscow like mad' and were no longer 'in it because of anything happening in the Soviet Union, but because of things we wanted to happen in Britain and elsewhere'.[9] John Lloyd, a former party member himself of course, sees that what Hobsbawm will never repudiate are the ideals of the movement he belonged to; the good intentions led to hell, but they were good intentions.[10] The lack of any defence of these ideals in *Interesting Times* and the great silences about the communist experience which Anderson found baffling, nevertheless leave Hobsbawm open to the charge, as Tony Judt puts it, of not learning from the tragedy of the twentieth century.

Richard Vinen also questions Hobsbawm's depiction of himself as a marginal figure.[11] By contrast to E. P. Thompson and other lone scholars he points out that Hobsbawm was always 'an institutions man', one of the few major historians of his generation who bothered to complete a PhD, 'a very English figure' who was 'at home in those gentlemen's clubs—the Apostles, the Athenaeum, the British Academy—that dominated twentieth-century English intellectual life'. Vinen also remarks on the 'Establishment's soft spot' for Hobsbawm, his great success in the capitalist world, and his appeal among the English middle classes, which, he says, puts him on a par with Elizabeth David (who introduced the suburbs to *French Provincial Cooking*). Vinen is not the only writer to see that Hobsbawm lost faith in party orthodoxy in the late 1950s. The *New Statesman* observed that the withdrawal from communism had begun even earlier—after 1956—even though he remained in the party, keeping the company of friends, his party-based political activity had virtually ceased. Hobsbawm's Marxism also withered away, according to the journal, doing little to inform his history of the twentieth century, and surviving only as 'a point of pride, a conceit'.[12] Vinen suspects a psychological explanation here but concedes that Hobsbawm himself emphasises politics, if only to avoid a reckoning with his past. Those with more active records of political engagement—Edward Thompson, for example—were, for Vinen, 'precisely those who felt most inclined to leave the party when they felt that it had betrayed the ideals for which they fought'. If there is something in this judgement, apart from ignorance—what of Margot Heinemann, for example?—it is not clear what. But then Vinen is disconcerted by Hobsbawm's tendency to 'veer away' from questions about his own political commitment, noting that 'the closer he comes to such questions, the more confusing he becomes'. The 'dynamic evasiveness' which Hobsbawm invokes when discussing American policy makers, he concludes, might just as well apply to himself.

The alleged evasiveness turns to self-promotion when Hobsbawm discusses British politics in the 1980s. Some reviewers also identify a 'lack of generosity' which, according to Anderson, 'disfgures' too many of his judgements. David Caute did not care for the sole anecdotal mention of Isaac Deutscher and wonders if Hobsbawm knew what Deutscher—and, for that matter, Orwell—were telling the world in the 1940s.[13] Anderson objects to the disparagement of Raphael Samuel and of Edward Thompson's political interventions and of the New Left generally. 'Scarcely an item in this sour retrospect withstands careful scrutiny'. 'Fatal delusion' enters the picture, for Anderson, in Hobsbawm's account of *Marxism Today*'s rescue of the Labour Party and his role in finishing off Tony Benn, while promoting the lamentable Kinnock. He reminds us that Hobsbawm, and others writing for (what *Scotland on Sunday*'s reviewer calls) 'the right-wing Marxist journal',[14] wanted a moderate leadership capable of attracting Middle England's votes. Well, they got it and now the Labour Left no longer exists. No doubt, this is not what they meant. Not what they wanted at all. But Anderson himself concludes on a generous note arguing that 'the abiding impression' left by this memoir 'is of the largeness of his mind and the complex distinction of the life it reports'.

Notes

1. *National Review*, 15 October, 2001.
2. Martin Amis, *Koba The Dread* (London, 2002), p.254.
3. Quoted in M. Jaggi, 'A Question of Faith', *Guardian*, 14 September 2002.
4. Perry Anderson, 'The Age of EJH', *London Review of Books*, 3 October 2002.
5. Niall Ferguson, 'What a swell party it was…for him', *Sunday Telegraph*, 20 October 2002.
6. *History Today*, January 1999.
7. *Observer*, 6 October, 2002.
8. Both cited in Jaggi, *Guardian*, 14 September 2002.
9. Ibid.
10. John Lloyd, *New Statesman*, 6 June 1997.
11. Richard Vinen, 'Dynamically evasive', *Times Literary Supplement*, 4 October 2002.
12. D. Lawday, 'Did France censor Hobsbawm?', *New Statesman*, 11 October 1999.
13. David Caute, 'Great helmsman or mad wrecker', *Spectator*, 19 October 2002.
14. D. Archibald, 'Radical historian tells it his way', *Scotsman on Sunday*, 13 October 2002.

An English Revolutionary
The work of Christopher Hill

Ann Hughes

Christopher Hill's paradoxical career combined a lifetime's commitment to socialist history, particularly of seventeenth-century England, with recognition by the British establishment of the most obvious sort as Master of Balliol College, Oxford, and Fellow of the British Academy. His death on 23 February 2003 was marked all over the world as well as in the British press, with the *Washington Post* (3 March 2003) describing him as 'a brilliant and controversial British-Marxist historian'. We are now so accustomed to a diet of 'popular history' that focuses overwhelmingly on war and scandal, kings and queens, that it is salutary to remember Hill's achievement in offering school students, and a broad public as well as professional scholars, a vision of English history that celebrated its revolutionary potential and the traditions of creative resistance by the common people. In 1952, Christopher Hill, with other socialist historians, played a major role in founding *Past and Present*, which remains the most prestigious English-language historical journal; his textbook, *The Century of Revolution* (1961), has offered generations of A- level students and undergraduates an alternative to high-political narrative, while works such as *The World Turned Upside Down. Radical Ideas in the English Revolution* (1972), and *Milton and the English Revolution* (1977), mobilised Hill's unequalled knowledge of the creative and polemical literature of the period to offer a rich account of heterodox speculation to a very wide audience.

Hill was the author of more than twenty books and innumerable articles; in attempting to sum up his influence I will focus on four aspects of his work on seventeenth-century England, especially the upheavals of the mid-century which he did so much to convince his readers amounted to an English Revolution. In the first place, he developed and made his own a broadly Marxist account of the 'English Revolution', working in the tradition of Marx, Engels and Bernstein. Hill always insisted that England experienced one of the great world revolutions, as significant as the French or Russian Revolutions; this was a bourgeois revolution, emerging within the tensions of feudalism, and facilitating the transformation to a capitalist society. The precise emphasis of Hill's argument has varied. In his *The English Revolution 1640* (1940), written on the eve of the Second World War, he argued that a new bourgeois class took power after overthrowing a feudal order maintained through capricious personal monarchy. In most later discussions, taking account of substantial research that revealed the complexity of social formations and allegiances in the civil wars of the 1640s, he presented a more structural account. The upheavals of the seventeenth century amounted to a bourgeois revolution not because they were willed by any class, but because they created the conditions for capitalist development. The new political structures secured the rights of the propertied classes, facilitated capitalist agriculture, and promoted overseas trade and commercial development. Crucial also was the defeat in the revolution of the more radical egalitarian movements who were increasingly Hill's focus.[1] In a wonderful essay, still worth taking heed of, and written (presumably) while Hill was still a member of the Communist Party, he stressed the need to relate legal and religious history to social development without interpreting events in 'crudely economic terms'.[2] A humane, open-minded, Marxist-influenced version of seventeenth-century English history characterises all Hill's work. In a late piece, commenting on the implications for historians of the fall of the Eastern European regimes in 1989–90, and tellingly entitled 'Premature obsequies', Hill claimed he had never been a Marxist in the sense that hostile questioners usually meant—of accepting 'a body of dogma to which I want to make history conform'. He admitted that the terms of his 1940 essay now seemed 'wholly inappropriate. I brandished the words "feudal" and "bourgeoisie" like weapons.' Nonetheless he was proud to describe himself as 'Marxist influenced' and although 'I have changed my vocabulary... I do not think I have shifted very far on my main "Marxist" point about 17th century England. I still think that the events between 1640 and 1660 are aptly described as a revolution, since they led to vast changes in the history of England and of the world.'[3] The nature of the English Revolution is of course controversial within Marxist scholarship, while influential elements of non-Marxist history would deny the label revolutionary altogether. Hill's consistent stress on the 1640s and 1650s as a major transformation in the history of England and the west has inspired much important historical work as well as much criticism.

Second, Hill always insisted that historical scholarship inspired or influenced by Marxism had to have a broad scope, and he followed this principle throughout his career. His illuminating studies of zealous Protestantism or Puritanism have influenced innumerable social and cultural historians. He understood the importance of the individual conscience, of the (to modern sensibilities unlikely) inspiration of a Calvinist sense of membership of an elect godly community, and the power of rousing sermons. He was always (controversially) insistent on the connection between religion (or other beliefs) and the material conditions of existence, seeing Puritanism as a crucial element in the lives of the 'middling sort' or the 'industrious sort of people', distinguishing them alike from rich and poor.[4] He wrote on the history of science, seeing affinities between Puritanism and a 'modern' experimental approach, and he had an abiding, and intimidatingly well-read concern with the connections between history and literature. Social changes and political preoccupations are inevitably imprinted in the literature of the period, and hence literary sources offer major opportunities for historians. Hill also wrote outstanding works on great 'canonical' figures of English literature, locating John Milton and John Bunyan in their complex social and ideological milieux, offering readers a striking picture of a heterodox, politically committed Milton in particular, closely involved in the radical speculation of the revolution.[5]

Third, from a remarkably early stage, but increasingly over his career, Christopher Hill uncovered in vivid case studies and more generally in perhaps his most influential work, *The World Turned Upside Down*, a history of the struggles and creative ideas of the common people. He insisted against many conservative social and political historians that early modern England was marked by class struggle and hostility, from the rich towards the poor as well as from poorer groups seeking to transform society.[6] He stressed the enduringly creative, radical capacity of the common people to criticise and struggle against the conditions of their oppression. An early and still cited essay, 'The Norman Yoke' (1954), written to honour the communist historian Dona Torr, outlined a radical and politically relevant version of English history as a struggle for the restoration of lost rights, while a later piece, 'Lollards to Levellers', posited an underground tradition of religious radicalism, underpinning an egalitarian social vision, found particularly in upland and forest areas of England.[7] *The World Turned Upside Down* dealt with the 'revolt within the Revolution', the outpouring of radical ideas that challenged the revolution of the respectable propertied parliamentarians who fought for limited monarchy, the rule of law and a reformed national church. Hill described how the breakdown of royal government, the violent splits in the governing elite and the end of censorship allowed the full flourishing of hitherto suppressed traditions of plebeian radicalism. It reflected the new preoccupations of socialists in the 1970s and 1980s, quoting Marcuse on revolution as a liberation of the imagination,[8] and besides discussions of economic struggles or the political manifestoes of parliament's radical army, Hill gave serious consideration to the utopian views of a range of prophets, mystics, and self-styled messiahs. He discussed 'Ranter' attacks on conventional concepts of sin and guilt, challenges to familial authority and touched, at least, on the struggles of women. His chapter, 'Base impudent kisses', dealt mostly it must be admitted with what radical ideas developed largely by men meant for women and the family, but also stressed that: 'The Revolution helped many women both to establish their own independence and to visualize a total escape for the poorer classes'.[9] This formulation reveals a characteristic faith in the capacity of socialism to transform all oppressive relationships, a faith not of course shared by all. Hill sought to rescue forgotten alternatives and to learn from those dismissed in their own time as the lunatic fringe: 'Lunacy, like beauty may be in the eye of the beholder... madness may be a form of protest against social norms...the 'lunatic' may in some sense be saner than the society which rejects him'.[10] Although *The World Turned Upside Down* can be seen as a product of the 1960s, it is remarkable looking back at the whole of Hill's career, how early he developed a pioneering interest in eccentric, fringe figures. His, now commonplace, argument, was that such figures reveal the norms and potential for alternative visions within societies; and he conducted much of this creative research while still a prominent figure amongst communist party historians. A typical example is his study of 'The mad hatter', Roger Crab, a vegetarian visionary and social critic of the 1640s and 1650s. Typically Hill associated him with perennial radical traditions—looking backwards to medieval ascetics like Francis of Assisi, and forward to nonconformist radicals who believed in 'individual self-mastery' as the basis for social change.[11] Throughout his career too he worked hard to make the radical writings of the seventeenth century available to modern readers. *The Good Old Cause* (1949), which he co-edited with Edmund Dell and was another project inspired by the Communist Party Historians' Group, offered a very broad selection of contemporary sources, while he also produced an important edition of the writings of the utopian communist Gerrard Winstanley.

Finally Hill had a proper, unostentatious but consistent sense of the necessary partisanship of the historian, a conviction that all attempts to make sense of the past are politically interested and politically relevant. This stance underlay his own work, but also fuelled his determined criticism of those who argued that the English civil war was a mere rebellion, or that the 'Ranters' were merely a media panic of the early 1650s, compounded by the Communist Party historians' search for a properly subversive movement in seventeenth-century England. Hill suffered throughout his life from the criticisms of scholars whose conviction of their own unpolitical 'objectivity' was as well developed as their capacity to detect Hill's bias, and he had no time for this claim to be unsullied by politics. In his textbook *The Century of Revolution* (1961) he insisted 'What happened in the seventeenth century is still sufficiently part of us today, of our ways of thinking, our prejudices, our hopes, to be worth trying to understand'.[12] His concern with radical ideas and movements, his challenges to revisionist accounts of the 'civil war' and his perennial energy in seeking to understand the variety of ways in which seventeenth-century England had a complex relevance for the present all came from a conviction that history mattered. *The World Turned Upside Down* in the early 1970s argued against patronising seventeenth-century radicals as 'ahead of their time', as they had not worked for 'our modern world, but something far nobler, something yet to be achieved—the upside-down world'. In the less optimistic 1980s he produced the deeply moving *The Experience of Defeat. Milton and Some Contemporaries* (1984) exploring how a variety of parliamentarians resisted or came to reluctant terms with, the dispiriting experience of the Restoration.

Hill faced criticism throughout much of his career, and indeed after his death with the implausible claims that he was a Soviet spy. The liberal American historian J. H. Hexter, denounced him as a 'lumper', not a 'splitter', someone who characteristically looked for (or exaggerated) connections rather than contradictions or anomalies. The links he forged between Puritanism and progressive ideas about science, or with particular social policies and identities can be regarded as too sweeping. He was deeply committed to a view of English popular culture as radical and subversive, and did not always give full attention to conservative or traditional attitudes amongst the people, or, for that matter, to the heterodox potential within elite culture. Paradoxically perhaps for a historian within Marxist traditions he did little research himself on social and economic history, relying on (and inspiring) the work of others in syntheses such as *The Century of Revolution* or *Reformation to Industrial Revolution*. He rarely, after 1940, engaged in public in elaborate theoretical debate, declaring in 1991, 'I have strong hangovers of English empiricism. I am not a political philosopher, just a historian interested in seventeenth-century England. I am chary of philosophical generalisations'.[13] Thus he did not contribute to the debate between Anderson and Thompson, for example, on the 'peculiarities of the English'.[14] We might consider this a strength or a weakness according to taste but Hill's good sense and wide knowledge of the seventeenth century might have made him a most productive contributor to these theoretical debates.

Re-reading Christopher Hill's works, I always find his account more sub-
tle and complex than his critics allow. In 'Recent Interpretations of the
English Civil War', for example, he acknowledged the importance of understanding popular royalism and of considering religious ideas in their own
right, and not merely as a 'cloak' for material concerns. He liked to make
connections between society and politics, or religion, culture and politics, and
he always saw the subversive potential in attitudes (such as Bunyan's) that
were sometimes more accommodating to earthly realities than he would have
hoped. Yet he usually stressed the exceptions and contradictions to the patterns he wove. Like many of the historians active in the communist party in
the 1940s and 1950s he combined a commitment to explaining overall
processes of historical change with an unwavering insistence on the capacity of people—'ordinary', unlettered and unprivileged people—to make their
own history, on the dogged resistance to economic exploitation and ideological mystification. In his work he demonstrated that all aspects of the past
should be the preserve of the radical scholar, writing illuminating studies of
Cromwell as well as Winstanley, Crab as well as Milton, Hobbes and
Clarendon as well as Abiezer Coppe the Ranter. His unparalleled knowledge
of the printed literature of the seventeenth century comprehending literary
works, religious treatises and political pamphlets has inspired several generations of literary scholars and historians. In his broader practice as a scholar,
Hill was a generous mentor to all those he found sympathetic (even where
they disagreed significantly with him on seventeenth-century history), and
well into his eighties he was an indefatigable speaker to student and adult
education groups as well as academic audiences. Above all he represented
an open-minded but determined conviction of the inevitable and productive connections between historical scholarship and present commitments.

Notes

1. For this version see his volume in the Penguin Economic History of England,
   Reformation to Industrial Revolution (Harmondsworth, 1967), or 'A bourgeois revolution?' (1980) in *The Collected Essays of Christopher Hill*, vol.3 (Brighton, 1986).
2. 'Recent Interpretations of the English Civil War' (1956), reprinted in *Puritanism
   and Revolution* (London, 1958).
3. 'Premature obsequies', *History Today*, April 1991, reprinted in Christopher Hill,
   England's Turning Point. Essays on Seventeenth-century English History (London, 1998).
4. See his *Society and Puritanism in Pre-Revolutionary England* (London, 1964).
5. *Milton and the English Revolution* (London, 1977); *A Turbulent, Seditious and Factious
   People: John Bunyan and his Church* (Oxford, 1988).
6. For the former see Hill, 'The many-headed monster in late Tudor and early

Stuart political thinking' in Charles H. Carter (ed.), *From the Renaissance to the Counter-Reformation. Essays in honour of Garrett Mattingly* (London, 1966).

7. Respectively reprinted in *Puritanism and Revolution* and Maurice Cornforth (ed.), *Rebels and their Causes: Essays in Honour of A. L. Morton* (London, 1978).

8. Christopher Hill, *The World Turned Upside Down* (Harmondsworth, 1975 edn), p.414.

9. Ibid, p.321.

10. Ibid. p.16.

11. Reprinted in *Puritanism and Revolution*, p.310.

12. Christopher Hill, *The Century of Revolution* (London, 1978 edn), p.13.

13. Hill, 'Premature Obsequies', p.292.

14. See E. P. Thompson, *The Poverty of Theory* (London, 1978); *Perry Anderson, Arguments within English Marxism* (London, 1980).

Christopher Hill and the Experience of Defeat

Martin Willis

Only a few days after his death, Christopher Hill was the subject of a short controversy across the op-ed and letters pages of a range of broadsheet papers. Not over the explanatory power of his analyses of the seventeenth century, though.

The fuss was over a claim that Hill was 'a Soviet mole'. Anthony Glees, Reader in Politics at Brunel University, provided the mix of fact, speculation and mischief which shaped the central article in *The Times*.[1] Glees noted that Hill served in Military Intelligence, then at the Foreign Office, during the Second World War. He suggested that this could only have been possible if Hill had 'concealed' his membership of the Communist Party of Great Britain (CPGB). Glees observed that Hill, in his official capacity, had made a number of proposals which were consistent with Soviet foreign policy. And he crowned his argument with a range of extremely tenuous attempts to associate Hill with a couple of figures who were later involved with espionage.

Although Glees had unearthed some previously classified information, such as policy papers showing that 'the department in which Hill worked had become convinced that Stalin would not pursue westward expansion of his empire into Central and Eastern Europe after the defeat of Germany', his views actually add up to nothing more than familiar facts presented as exposé, and ahistorical attempts to present sympathy with the Soviet Union as irrefutable evidence of wrong-headedness and 'treachery'.

In reality, the fact that Hill joined the CPGB in the mid-1930s, and that 'during the war he served in the Army and then at the Foreign Office (due to his knowledge of Russian and the Soviet Union)' has always been widely known.[2] As Nick Cohen observed during the Glees-provoked controversy, Hill's politics had been well publicised at the beginning of the war. His first book, *The English Revolution*, had been put out by the official CPGB publishing house Lawrence and Wishart in 1940, attracting a scathing review from George Orwell who noted its explicit and, at that early stage in Hill's career, somewhat one-dimensional Marxism. For Cohen, this episode illustrated how unlikely it was that Hill was anything other what he seemed to be: 'Real moles hide everything. They last thing they would do is send out communist tracts to be reviewed in the *New Statesman* by hostile critics who would point out their communism as a matter of course.'[3]

More generally, Glees stands poorer as a reader of political history for not having acknowledged that the combination of being communist and working for the war effort was not uncommon, even at fairly high levels in the military and in intelligence. And part of the reason for this was that, from June 1941, the Soviet Union and Britain were allies! Hill was not the only one making suggestions consistent with Soviet foreign policy.

Taking a kick

On the basis of such contextualisation, many might conclude that there is nothing of much interest, let alone anything scandalous or improper, about Hill's wartime activities. Serving in the machinery of the British state in this period and promoting the political cause he supported were entirely consistent.

It is therefore more interesting to take Glees's reading of Hill's career as illustrating current forms of anti-communism in British intellectual life. References to the communist movement are routinely designed to reinforce a notion that it was monolithic, inherently totalitarian and oppressive. This trend involves grotesque conflations of all wings and forms of communism, at all times and in all places. It is an attempt to deny that major currents in the movement were often drivers of democratic change.

Why, though, do such views still need pushing in such places as *The Times*? There is hardly a red threat today. Some see an ongoing campaign to discredit the possibility of any progressive alternative to the current neo-liberal capitalist ascendancy, part of what Zizek has helped identify as the reactionary 'project of *disutopia*: not just the temporary absence of Utopia, but the celebration of the end of social dreams'.[4]

Using the fact that the twentieth-century communist project ended in failure, opponents of progressive social transformation are insisting that it was always bound to fail. And they are going further, arguing that all such attempts are always going to be bound to fail.

Others see ongoing work to discredit the communist experience as a way of distracting attention from the manifest social failures and horrors thrown up by today's settlements. If supporters of neo-liberal globalisation want to console themselves in relation to the fact that a range of problems are not only unsolved through its workings, but are generated and made worse, what better than to take another satisfying kick at the defeated historical alternative?

All this shows the need for continuing work to illustrate and insist on the varied and contradictory nature of the twentieth-century communist movement. It should actually be presented as taking in a range of movements, which embodied and worked for a wide spectrum of different political contents and interests. And the job of exploring the extent to which options and possibilities were *open* at different points in the movement's history is linked to the task of arguing that, when a potentially successful progressive social-transformative movement rises again, it need not end in tyrannies and failures.

Perhaps this will involve a little spat with Glees over the question of whether Hill and his Foreign Office colleagues may not, after all, have been correct in their assessment of Stalin's ambitions in 1943 and 1944. After all, and setting aside the withdrawal of Soviet troops from Austria and Stalin's proposal that Germany be constituted as united but neutral, the post-war 'westward expansion' of the Soviet 'empire' was at least in part a defensive response to the hegemonic intent of the USA's Marshall Plan.

Their trade was loyalty

Reassessments of the twentieth-century communist movement will need to engage with the fact that a number of communists in capitalist countries did act as spies, for the Soviet Union and for other 'actually existing socialist states'. For some, this was unglamorous, mundane and low-profile activity. Sometimes, as with the Burgess and Maclean circle, it involved high-level, risky, sustained deception, in which they had to work hard to hide their true political identity. Together with the fact that they worked directly and effectively against the interests of 'their own' country in favour of a 'foreign power', this explains why associating others with them is an easy way of stimulating excitement and popular condemnation.[5]

But a dispassionate account of the period in which the main cohort of Soviet agents was recruited allows us to see that simple or sensationalist judgements are misplaced. Hobsbawm has recently reiterated his view that the 1930s was a period in which 'patriotism, in the sense of automatic loyalty to a citizen's national government' counted for little. 'When the Second World War ended, the governments of at least ten old European countries were headed by men who at its beginning...had been rebels, political exiles or, at the very least, who had regarded their own governments as immoral and illegitimate.'[6] In a context in which the Soviet Union seemed the only consistent opponent of Nazism, and where international communism attracted and shaped the hopes of hundreds of thousands of young people, many determined that their real allegiance was to the cause they had chosen, rather than to the often discredited state running things where an accident of birth had delivered them. 'The lines of loyalty…ran not between but across countries'.

The issue then became one of how they would serve that cause. Only a very small number were approached to do so through espionage. Some of those who were approached declined. But, again according to Hobsbawm, most communists then and into the subsequent decades 'knew such work was going on, we knew we were not supposed to ask questions about it, we respected those who did it, and most of us—certainly I—would have taken it on ourselves, if asked'.

Ten years after the dissolution of the CPGB, Hobsbawm can afford to be so candid. Through the decades in which it established itself and operated as a credible national political force, the usual public line of the party was to distance itself entirely from Soviet agents, and to criticise if not to condemn their work as being an improper and unhelpful way to pursue the cause.

There's little doubt that this straightforward line was for public consumption, rather than expressing the rather more complex private feelings of most communist leaders and intellectuals. It was the necessary position for an organisation wanting to articulate socialism as a patriotic vision, the best possible future for the vast majority of Britons. And it was a line which was necessary in order to defend the party's credentials and rights as a democratic and legal organisation operating within the institutions and parameters established by the British state.

It was also an expression of the strong views of those communist leaders who had come to be primarily focussed on the interests and tasks of their own parties, which they had worked to establish as legitimate actors in national political contexts. After having to cope with the fallout of leading party members Percy Glading and Dave Springhall being convicted for inept spying efforts in 1938 and 1943 respectively, it is almost certain that the CPGB leadership neither took part in nor were asked to take part in any recruitment of agents. However, there is little evidence that they had ever done so: even in the days of 'class against class', when they put aside any thoughts of articulating the party's politics in terms of an alternative version of 'the national interest'.

The wartime case, in particular, infuriated the then general secretary Pollitt, who spent the night of Springhall's conviction walking the streets and cursing the Russians. 'What, after all, did they care for his efforts to establish communism in Britain if they could behave in so scandalous and irresponsible a fashion?'[7] This does not necessarily mean that Pollitt or the CPGB leadership disapproved of spying in principle, but that he was infuriated by the way that the Soviet Union could use the party (particularly its national organiser!) in a way that could only inflict political damage on it at home.[8] Where party members combined or replaced their legal activities with work for the Soviet Union or other states, it seems clear that an approach came directly from those states, or involved the freelance initiative of the spies themselves. There is no evidence of any direct connection between their secret life and the CPGB itself.

Minority report

None of which has anything whatsoever to do with the activities or career of Christopher Hill. The preposterous story about him being a 'traitorous' spy tempts us to get confused about what was important about his work and political activity, and to get things out of proportion.

The debates we continue to need about Hill are about his judgements on Cromwell and the Levellers, and the social dynamics of 'the century of revolution'. A fair starting point for evaluating Hill's contribution is Cohen's comment that 'more than any other historian in the twentieth century, he showed how ordinary people developed ideas of democracy, socialism, secularism and women's emancipation as soon as [the English] civil war destroyed censorship and political control and allowed them the space to think and argue'.[9]

Any more general assessment of Hill's life must centre on his work and style as an organiser of academic life, and on his periods of political activity. In one of these, proposing a minority report on how the CPGB might have re-organised after the dramatic events of 1956, Hill briefly found himself a leader of a political tendency which, with just a bit more resource, could have brought together the creativity and democratic commitment of the emerging new left, a serious approach to discipline, organisation and alliance building, and significant numbers of activists. Who knows how such a force might have helped shape the 1960s and subsequent decades?

Notes

1. Ian Cobain, 'Was Oxford's most famous Marxist a Soviet mole?', *The Times*, 5 March 2003.
2. Harvey Kaye, *The British Marxist Historians* (Basingstoke, 1995 edn), p. 102.

3. Nick Cohen, *Observer*, 9 March 2003.

4. Slavoj Zizek, 'Afterword: Lenin's choice' in Zizek (ed.), *Revolution at the Gates: A selection of writings from February to October 1917* by V. I. Lenin (London, 2002), p.168.

5. In May 2003, the BBC 2 television drama series *The Cambridge Spies*, written by Peter Moffat, provided a focus for discussion on this circle.

6. Eric Hobsbawm, *Interesting Times. A twentieth-century life* (London, 2002), p.102.

7. Kevin Morgan, Harry Pollitt (Manchester, 1993), pp.178–9.

8. In a speech which contrasted Springhall's record in Spain with that of the appeasers, Pollitt claimed in January 1944: 'Our Party dealt with Springhall immediately his trial was ended, not because we knew what he had done, but because we consider it indefensible that any member of the Communist Party could place himself in a position which could be used against the Party by the bitterest enemies of the working class.' He did not condemn the passing of information to the Russians as such, but made the rather different claim, that no member of the CPGB had 'done a single action calculated to help the Fascist enemy' (*Daily Worker*, 21 January 1944).

9. *Observer*, 9 March 2003.

Cambridge Communism in the 1930s and 1940s

Reminiscences and reflections

The association of Cambridge with the communism of the 1930s remains perennially in the public eye. Certain images predominate. One, of course, is that of spies: of Burgess, Maclean and those whose exposure followed, either muddying the waters of the decade's commitments or else showing how deeply ran the impulse to 'take sides'. Another image, perhaps the other side of the coin, is that of John Cornford: poet, communist and symbol of the generation that fought in Spain—though, as Eric Hobsbawm points out in his memoirs, the Communist Party did not encourage students to go to Spain and few went.[1] Emerging over the longer term, Cambridge between the early 1930s and mid-1940s also produced a remarkable cohort of left-wing intellectuals, of whom Hobsbawm was only one. Others, to name only those familiar as historians to readers of this journal, included Victor Kiernan, Edward Thompson, Dorothy Thompson and—if we think of his major writings on the history of education—Brian Simon.

As the following reminiscences show, they were not all future historians, nor indeed were they all spies, poets or Apostles. Taken from materials collected for a broader biographical project on British communism, these recollections provide, not so much a detailed record of Cambridge communism, as a sense of the different routes by which young people found their way to communism in a decade dominated by the issues of slump, fascism and war. These eleven individuals—even the brother and sister among them—all got to Cambridge, and to communism, from different starting points. Between them they give a sense of the social cleavages that divided Britain, and of the ways in which educational opportunities were both structured by gender and social class, and then in turn—though this will not of course be so obvious from the lives of those who got to Cambridge—helped perpetuate the same divisions.

The recollections can be left to speak for themselves, but perhaps three preliminary comments can be made. The first is that their social origins range considerably widely than some accounts would lead one to expect. Recently Stephen Woodhams has questioned the stress placed by earlier writers like Neal Wood on the link between Oxbridge communism and the more exclusive public schools.[2] Brian Harrison, in an article on Oxford socialism, has also identified communism in this period with 'the public-school undergraduate in revolt'.[3] The accounts presented here, though providing some support for such an interpretation (notably an old Etonian), suggest that it is little more than a stereotype, no doubt encouraged by the same prevailing images of Cornford, Burgess and Maclean. For at least some Cambridge communists of the war years, the attraction of the party branch was precisely its feeling of otherness from the more established university milieux in which they found they scarcely belonged.

But of course, those perceptions, and the branch itself, changed over time. Viewed in a longer perspective, these accounts seem to fit together as part of a common generational experience: compared with the students of the 1950s, and still more those of the 1920s, the heyday of Cambridge communism stands out as a clearly delineated moment of its own. Viewed closer up, however, it is also clear that the annual replenishment of the student body meant that political and social changes were registered with an immediacy not usually found in more settled populations. Socially, in this decade the door of educational opportunity was ever so slightly opening wider: particularly perhaps with regard to gender, for of course our images of spies, Apostles and even International Brigaders are all very much masculine ones. More dramatically, this was also a decade in which politically both communism and international events periodically revealed aspects and alignments that seemed to turn the world upside down. The most obvious shift is that from issues of unemployment and peace—two of the earlier recall the impact of *All Quiet on the Western Front*—to that of anti-fascism. In his memoirs Hobsbawm suggests a more fundamental reorientation, which he dates to around 1935, from a concept of world revolution, focused on the USSR, to what we would now think of as the politics of the popular front. In the context in which Hobsbawm mentions it—that of his remaining in the Communist Party when others left in 1956—it certainly seems significant that by the late 1930s joining the party often seems to have meant suppressing certain reservations about the USSR. In all three cases included here—John Maynard Smith, Dorothy Wedderburn and Peter Worsley—that had the corollary of leaving the party in 1956.

On the other hand, Hobsbawm's case also suggests the care with which such distinctions need to be handled, for though he joined the Communist Party in England in 1936, he first thought of himself as a communist in

Berlin in 1932. That suggests a third reflection, and perhaps the most surprising one: that of these individuals, a majority were politically active before they went to Cambridge and four were members of the Communist Party or Young Communist League. The relative longevity of their political commitments means that these no doubt were untypical: there must have been many more—like the future high court judge mentioned by George Barnard—for whom communism was more specifically a sort of student rite of passage. In terms of the old conundrum of whether the East End made Jews red, or Jews made the East End red, it does seem that in many cases it was the students who made Cambridge red and not the other way round. In a decade in which gifted and highly motivated young people were often drawn towards communism, Cambridge perhaps provided a catalyst and political space, where a critical mass of such activists, combined with the assiduous attentions of the party itself, swept along those who otherwise would probably never have become communists.

Thanks are due to all those involved in assisting with their recollections. Victor Kiernan, John Maynard Smith and Dorothy Thompson provided written recollections, the others were interviewed for the CPGB biographical project and the recordings are now available in the National Sound Archive.[4] The interviewers were Francis King (Ralph Russell) and Kevin Morgan, who who also wrote the introduction. The interviews were edited for style and continuity.

Victor Kiernan
Trinity College 1931–7

My parents were both born and bred in Manchester, both long-lived, both with Irish roots. I wish I had tried to learn more about them. My mother's ancestors, over many years, were farmers in Ulster, and presbyterians. My father's father had more of a wandering life, with a story of running away in boyhood when his family fell into penury, and trying to walk to Scotland, and catch a sheep. He joined the army, served in Hong Kong and then in the conquest of Egypt in 1882; worked in the mills, and for years was a trade union representative—simply, I think, because he was a teetotaller, and could be regarded as reliable.

My father grew up in a Wesleyan Methodist family. He wished he could have been a scholar, and was a good deal a self-educated man, who could remember wearing clogs. A cousin became a Methodist minister. My father learned Spanish and Portuguese at night-school, where he later taught, and his firm sent him to Lisbon for six months. After marriage he moved to another neighbourhood and another church, the Congregational. He always had a melancholy temperament, as he once told me. To attend a church service on Sunday mornings was a firm habit with him, but he shrank from getting involved in any church activities, and joined a congregation distant enough to give him an excuse to keeping to himself. I was taken to listen to sermons and hymns when much too young to benefit by them. More willingly I was taken to watch cricket matches, on the famous Old Trafford ground not far from which I grew up.

My mother's family were faring better. Two brothers were partners in a building enterprise, which did well for a good many years, but failed to move with the times, and collapsed. My mother was left on Sundays to housework and children, and her religion was chiefly an inherited dislike of Catholics. Later in life she used to attend the services of one of the first women preachers who gathered a congregation. The family had few friends, even acquaintances. My mother was the loser by this; my father would close the door on a departing visitor with a sigh of relief, and go back to his books, of which he collected a fair number. I reacted against parental prejudices, sympathising with the Irish cause, and even tolerating Catholicism. My mother had little sense of humour, unlike my father, who had a great many amusing stories; she had fits of gloom which she wanted her three children to sympathise with. She was a Tory, but thought poorly of all clergymen and politicians; my father was a Liberal. I did not go out into the world with any wish for a family of my own.

I was born in 1913 and attended the Manchester Grammar School, then at the crowded close of its four centuries in the town centre. There I got to know other pupils, and competed with the smarter ones, and liked some of the teachers, though not those who tried to teach me mathematics. I was on the classical side, with other elements, among them French, with Latin and Greek. But in my last three years I was persuaded by a more strong-willed youth to change into a newly founded 'History Sixth', under a young Cambridge man anxious for us to do him credit. Later on we were largely self-taught, left to go out and forage in the neighbouring libraries. I ought to have been getting more interested in politics by that time, but was floating too much among literary clouds, especially the romantic poets who were most in league with nature. In my last spell I won three scholarships, a Major at Trinity College, Cambridge and a State and a County. These ought to have made me rich, but they were added up and reduced to £220 p.a. My diary reminds me that the first question in my first exam paper at Trinity, in piercingly cold December weather, was 'Who were the Greeks?' I went up to Trinity in 1931.

I looked forward with some trepidation to Cambridge, and to having to wear a dinner-jacket. I did acquire one, but was relieved some years later by losing it on a journey, and receiving insurance money; I never bought another. No doubt I have remembered the following years more vividly than most because they brought the biggest change. In the first year I felt some spells of Wordsworthian solitariness; but there were numbers of MGS students within hail. They held occasional meetings, one with a lecture on questions of sex. Religion had left a faint afterglow, soon to be displaced by socialism.

I was lodged in a rather dingy corner of Whewell's Court, a nineteenth-century addition made by a Master of that name, in a ground-floor pair of small rooms (I.2) close to the gateway opening on to Jesus Lane. There was a coal fire, which when the wind blew overhead filled the place with volumes of smoke that drove me out into the fresh air. I stayed here longer than I need have done, into my fourth year when I changed to a top-floor dwelling over the main entrance to Great Court, with its fountain playing musically, especially on moonlit nights. At home late nights had always been discouraged; I could now indulge in the luxury of sitting up reading till well after midnight, though it was not long before I discovered the unwholesome side of this. I began keeping a diary, and resolved to compose at least a hundred lines of verse each month. Few of these had any claim to merit, though they provided a training in methods and metres.

My corner of the college was a not undistinguished one. It included a Russian, Count Sologub, related to the well-known writer; he was amiable and interesting to listen to, and a linguist, like all Russians of the old school. At an opposite pole was James Klugmann, who was coming to the front in the Communist Party, which seemed to have more members than I expected to see. I used to run into him coming home late from a meeting where he had been 'putting the party line': one evening baffled by a super-subtle Jesuit chaplain, Father D'Arcy, with his distinctions between 'Probabilism', 'Probabiliorism', etc. By day he could be seen in the college grounds, fencing. Incongruously close to Klugmann was the poet and Latinist A.E. Housman, who avoided all the company he could, like Wittgenstein later. High above my head was a student from Derbyshire, already a political arguer. One day I saw a piano being hoisted in through his window—he played very modern and very loud music, whereas my taste in all the arts was severely classical.

I liked to break off my work, when it grew tedious, for a stroll in the Backs, with the tortuous river Cam; splendid especially in spring with the long lines of daffodils, or in November (when I first saw them, for the scholarship exam) with the willows drooping over the misty water. Students holding scholarships had the privilege of playing a game of bowls along the river's edge, with some risk of the ball disappearing in the water. At one time boomerang throwing was in vogue. As I grew bolder I learned to punt. But my best occupation, when not reading, was to go out on Sunday mornings on my cycle, when I acquired a second-hand machine, and explore the placid scenery of Cambridgeshire.

By my second year I was able to feel more at ease, especially when alone. October was a fine month of paling sunlight, and at teatime I sat in my arm-chair, looking up at the sky, after arduously toasting some bread over the fire, and read for the first time Boswell's *Hebrides*, with the accompaniment of a single weekly cigarette—which however soon began to multiply, and formed a habit that took many years to shake off.

The Master of Trinity when I arrived was J. J. Thomson, who discovered the electron. He was old now, and his false teeth were said to rattle when he gave a speech, athough I was assured that in meetings of the college coun-cil he was still quite businesslike. G. M. Trevelyan, who was to succeed him, was then Regius Professor of History. He did little lecturing, but was care-ful to make the acquaintance of even the most junior of Faculty members. I was twice given lunches alone with him in my later years at the College, and on one occasion taken by him and his chauffeur to see the patch of ancient Fenland which he had helped to save from being drained. It was then, with war looming, that he said he would be ready to die, if that could avert an explosion. Since then I have seen him described as an awful snob; if so, he was good at disguising it.

A student was sent each term to one of the college's available 'supervi-sors', who was supplied with a list of subjects for essays; one of these he gave the student, to write on during the week. When he came back he was asked to read it aloud; this disposed of half of the half-hour (occasionally three-quarters), and the teacher then gave his comments or criticisms. The procedure was wasteful of time; during or after the war it was given up and the supervisor had to read all the essays handed in—with a good deal of grumbling at the extra work.

Among the seniors of my time F. A. Simpson had had a high reputation for his Anglican sermons, and acquired an aeroplane to fly him about; but he was now ageing and irascible; he disliked this work, though he still enjoyed lecturing, on the Eastern Question. Reginald de Vere Laurence taught medieval economic life. He suffered from gout, and I might find him heav-ily bandaged, and surrounded with a regiment of empty bottles on the carpet round him. Nonetheless, he could make useful comments. He was one of a small group of the same generation who met regularly to eat, drink and be merry. One was Gow, a Latinist and my not unhelpful 'tutor' or manager. He smiled when I asked him one day whether he had composed the Latin valediction to Lawrence as a companion' 'iocundissimus', which I had found inscribed somewhere in the college. Lapsley was an American, a medievalist, who lived for his weekly lecture to a large audience in the Hall; it was given without visible notes. He was said to collect photographs of himself with members of the aristocracy; but I remember a morning when I had cycled up the river in preparation for an examination, and met him: he got off his cycle, and gave me a few words of encouragement. Of the younger men one was a Catholic, a good pianist but not an outstanding historian. The one who made most stir, in his early thirties, liked to figure as 'George Kitson Clark'; malicious tongues said that his name was really plain Clark. He was a Tory of Tories; Klugmann told me that he liked to call on him now and then and frighten him with predictions of the revolution coming to swallow him up. I went to the chapel to hear him preach, along with some other jokers. He made three points—life in Cambridge was very pleasant; unfortunately few could share in it; the rest therefore must look forward to rewards due to them in heaven.

Most of the quad were bachelors, which may have had something to do with their stationary outlook. Attendance at lectures, or at a certain percentage of them, was compulsory. I compiled notes on them assiduously, but when revising for exams it was my notes on books that I turned to. It was to a galaxy of eminent scientists that the college owed its repute. Apart from them, I could see some point in the very early verdict of a fellow-Mancunian, who had been headboy of the school: 'Cambridge is a ramp'—in other words, an imposture. As a scholar I could attend all the lavish banquets that took place annually, and could not help feeling that they were far too extravagant, whereas the servitors looked ill-nourished. The slump of the 1930s made cheap labour easily available.

My diary shows me very unpolitical in my first year; I seem seldom to have read newspapers. In the summer of 1931 Ramsay MacDonald abandoned Labour and won an election with a right-wing coalition. In a crowd gathered at the Union to hear the election results read out I was innocent enough to join in the loud clapping for his own success; it was not to be long before I was part of a demonstration through the streets, singing 'We'll hang Ramsay Mac upon a sour apple-tree'.

Economic conditions helped to speed education. University advisers on jobs tried to steer young men towards the army, but there were growing doubts as to what the army was to be used for. In a college magazine where Inevitably progressive students soon began to divide between socialists and communists: a pity, in retrospect, because it weakened both. The more extreme had a stiffening in the Jewish contingent including a swelling number of refugees, chiefly from Germany. Klugmann had a brother-in-law in Maurice Cornforth, who was becoming a prominent Marxist philosopher; early on, a too rigid one. I spent a night listening to a ding-dong argument between Klugmann and the socialist leader McAlpine, an impressively tall young man who was learning to be a competent speaker. It ended inconclusively, at daybreak, with slices of cake. Socialists complained, with some reason, that their rivals were trying to steamroller them. One such was Douglas Smith, a Welshman, who devoted his last years to Welsh history instead of mathematics. After leaving college he was himself for a time a communist, and also did much for the co-operative movement. John Cornford, later killed in Spain, was the son of a professor of classical philosophy, belonging to the college, and a poetess mother.[5] Perhaps this parentage stimulated the opposite side of his nature, as a man of action. A schoolmate of his told me many years later that John was a man born for battle, a fighter in the most physical sense.

Still, theory meant much to him as well as practice, and I got to know him best when we were arguing about the Marxist theory of history, on which I had many reservations. In organisation the communists were the most advanced group. They sought recruits by winning the individual, not only the generality. This was called 'contact work': in each college 'cell' each member was commissioned to give special attention to the student he knew best, and, perhaps with a partner, bring him to feel that the only right place for him was the party. He was often surprised when he found what had been happening to him. Regular joint meetings were held, to discuss progress; attendance was divided into two categories: 'activists', always present, and others, not always for some reason able to take so big a part. Contingents from the women's colleges were meanwhile joining the socialists or the communists, and taking part in their doings.

Klugmann, whom I got to know well, was a past-master in what might be called the tricks of the trade, for manoeuvring people so as to get them doing things without letting them know what was happening. I sometimes felt some uneasiness over these well-meant devices, and outsiders might smell an un-British rat. In my time as a Fellow I was once called on to go round all the other Fellows (nearly a hundred—a day's work) and ask for signatures to a petition on behalf of some political prisoners abroad. I began with the Master, now G. M. Trevelyan. He had evidently come to feel that communist schemes might not be what appeared on the surface. He signed, as a good Liberal, but after asking me to give him my word of honour that there was no trickery involved. I hope there wasn't. I disliked nothing more than being asked to go round knocking at strangers' doors, in college or on the streets, just as I disliked people knocking on *my* door; one day when faced with this business I was vastly relieved when I began by calling on the excellent Douglas Smith to ask for some advice: I found him in a state of depression, and to shake it off he volunteered to take over the whole responsibility.

Another part of our education came with the hunger marchers passing through Cambridge. We went out for some miles to join up with them; female students undertook most of the arrangements for their night's stay. I joined the *party*, which meant the Communist Party—as distinct from the worthless Labour Party, as we deemed it—in November 1934, and stayed in it, though with increasingly mixed feelings, for 25 years. Historians were likely to stay in longer than most, though along with a number of scientists. One member very active in Cambridge came back from a wartime spell in India transformed into a mystical Hindu; India had converted him, instead of the other way round.

About this time I remember being given a lunch—in the conservative Pitt Club, which seemed a little incongruous—by Guy Burgess, whom I knew slightly as belonging to the Trinity cell. We discussed the Marxist theory of history, which was the staple of a good many debates I had with John Cornford. I felt a good many difficulties about it; and when I was applying for a research scholarship, and went to see two pillars of the Establishment, Sir John Clapham the economic historian, and Temperley the expert on diplomatic history, I told them I was looking for a subject that would enable me to decide about Marxist history. The outcome was a three-year study of western imperialism in China, which at least brought me a four-year fellowship.

It also brought me a commission from the party to get in touch with a small group of Indians who had been showing an interest in socialism, and one or two of whom evolved into active party members when back in India. I was able also to get to know a few members of the Chinese community, and one or two Africans. Cambridge housed quite a population of these exotics, and in Cambridge, if not at home under British rule, they seemed to be treated as complete equals. Several Indians made their mark as orators in the Union debates.

I have scarcely seen Cambridge for half a century, and know very little about what it is like now. I do not regret my long stay there, or my longer stay in the party. Its goal, a revolutionary change in all social and political relations was, in Britain in our day, an impossibility, as became growingly evident. But it could on the other hand claim a good many lesser achievements; and its corporate life could bring with it a good many compensations.

After returning to Trinity College as a Fellow after the Second World War, Victor Kiernan had a distinguished academic career and is now Professor Emeritus of Modern History at Edinburgh University. His books include The Lords of Human Kind, State and Society in Europe, 1550–1650 *and* Duelling in European History. *His two articles on Cambridge in the 1930s, 'Herbert Norman's Cambridge' and 'On treason', were reprinted in his* Poets, Politics and the People *(London, 1989); He left the CPGB in 1959.*

Roger Simon
Gonville and Caius College 1932–5

I was born in Manchester in October 1913 and brought up in Manchester too, except that I went to a public school. My father Ernest Simon took over from his father a very successful engineering business, which he had set up when he came over to Manchester from Germany in 1860. However, after a certain stage he decided that he wouldn't devote more than half of his time to the business, and that the other half would be devoted to public affairs. He went into local government and in 1920 he become Lord Mayor of Manchester at an unusually early age. My mother, Shena Simon, was also active in local politics and went on to the Manchester education committee, where she stayed for a very long time; so I was brought up in this atmosphere of public service. My father was a Liberal MP for the two short parliaments, the Labour governments of 1923–4 and 1929–31, and when he lost his seat he devoted himself to all sorts of other causes. My mother had joined the Labour Party in 1935, and eventually at the end of the war he did too.

There was a lot of politics at home and friends of the family included people like Sir Walter Layton, the editor of the *News Chronicle*, and John Scott, who was manager of the *Manchester Guardian*. The school I went to, Gresham's School, Holt, was favoured by various Liberal families, like the Laytons and the Floods. James Klugmann was there, although he was in a different house from me, and Donald Maclean was in my house, although he was slightly older. Then I went to Cambridge just when the student movement was gathering power. However, I didn't join the Communist Party until after I left. I studied economics, so I was much influenced by Keynes, who was a dominating influence there; and of course, according to Keynes's principles you could eliminate unemployment by public expenditure, so that the argument that unemployment was an essential feature of capitalism didn't quite work for me.

Also, I suppose that I didn't meet the right people. My younger brother Brian joined the CP in November 1934, but he was in Trinity College, which was where James Klugmann was. I was in Gonville and Caius, which seemed to be rather full of rugby players and medical students: very conservative people. Quite early on I did go to a meeting of the Socialist Society at which George Lansbury was speaking. Some people in the audience were very rude to him, and I thought he was a terribly nice man and I was put off by this and stopped going to the Socialist Society. I was really a sort of Liberal, or social democrat, but gradually I think the Communist Party seemed to be the only party which was trying to do something about unemployment and trying to do something about fascism and war. I also read a book by Harold Laski, *The State in Theory and Practice*, which was very good about the state really being an instrument of the capitalist class. Maurice Dobb was there, of course, but I think he had to be very careful and consequently he delivered a set of lectures on industrial relations which was terribly dull. But I did go to one or two talks by him, and some friends of mine joined the Communist Party, and that all had an effect on me. Then just after graduating I went on a visit to the Soviet Union and met Emile Burns on the boat coming back. The impressions I had were very favourable and I think it was at that time that I decided that I was a communist.

After working as a solicitor in local government, Roger Simon in 1958 went to work unpaid at the Labour Research Department, living on a parental legacy. He was secretary of the LRD from 1965 to 1977 and worked part-time there until shortly before his death in 2002. He remained a member of the Communist Party until 1991 and was subsequently a member of the Green Socialist Network.

George Barnard
St John's College 1933–7

I was born in Walthamstow in 1915. My father was a cabinet-maker but he was unemployed from around the time of the General Strike. He had been the local shop steward in his company, F. H. Eyres, the sports equipment manufacturers, and there was a strike on there which he thought he ought to support and was rewarded by losing the job that he had had for well over twenty years. After that he occasionally got temporary jobs as a joiner. Cabinet making essentially died out as a trade by 1930 or 1931, but the building trade was tending to pick up, and he worked as a joiner or a carpenter, though he didn't get any steady work until the rearmament boom when he worked on making the *mosquitos*, the wooden aeroplanes.

Really I was born and bred as a socialist. My father was a member of the Labour Party who took the *Daily Herald* and was quite an active supporter.

Also, William Morris was a Walthamstow man and was made much of locally: in fact the borough motto is 'Fellowship is Life', which is a quote from Morris. I can remember going to the William Morris Hall, the local headquarters of the Labour Party, and seeing a film of Lenin's funeral after he died in 1924. Walthamstow was a marvellous place to grow up in then. I went to the local grammar school, the St George Monoux Grammar School, and one of the advantages was that the borough was very well provided with local scholarships to help people go to university. In fact, my mother was keen that I should try and get a job as soon as I was old enough but my father was keen that I should take whatever scholarships were available and I was able to show her that I would get enough scholarships to be able to pay her more than I would have been able to if I had got a job. I was only the second one from my school to go to Cambridge, though we had had about three or four previously who went to Oxford.

I had already got interested in politics in Walthamstow in 1931 when the National Government was formed. First of all I joined the ILP. They used to have regular speakers on Saturday nights and for several months I went along to their meetings. The branch was split and I was in the Revolutionary Policy Committee which then joined the Communist Party. That was in 1932 that I reckoned myself a member, so I joined the Communist Party at the age of sixteen.

The CP was altogether different from the ILP. For one thing the ILP was a group of about five or six people, they didn't have the same international links. A very important factor for me at that time was the 1914–18 war and the slaughter that had occurred. All of this was carefully hidden until the publication of Remarque's book, *All Quiet on the Western Front*, and then the truth came out and there was an enormous reaction that nothing like that should ever happen again. Therefore a party which claimed to be a world party, with the slogan *Workers of the World, Unite!*, was very appealing; you were a member of the Communist International, you weren't just a member of the Communist Party here, and once a month you paid your dues to the international, not the local party. I remember having a friend who, when it was pointed out that there weren't a lot of communists about, always used to reply that he was a member of the largest political party in the world.

The situation in Germany was then developing quite fast. I remember being worried because the KPD was bitterly opposed to whoever was the socialist candidate for chancellor and fielded their own candidate Thaelmann. That of course let Hitler in and I remember thinking they were a bit sectarian. Russia wasn't so important in my becoming a communist. My father had taken me to a Labour Party meeting at which a chap from Russia came and talked about what was happening there, and there were two school-teachers I knew very well who were both very active with the Friends of the Soviet Union. But the general attitude in Walthamstow was that the communists were really just a ginger group, very keen and very active and so on. The party members were very mixed. There were ordinary working-class people with ordinary jobs, quite a few unemployed, and one or two city clerks, because quite a lot of people took the train from Walthamstow to Liverpool Street. My clearest recollection is celebrating the fiftieth anniversary of the death of Karl Marx in March 1933. I had already read *The Communist Manifesto*, and eventually at Cambridge I got as far as the third volume of *Capital*. Certainly you were expected to know the first.

I went to Cambridge in 1933 and read mathematics at St John's College. As I was already a party member I immediately got in touch with the local communists and we met in rooms in Magdalene belonging to A.R.H.T. Cumming-Bruce, who subsequently became a very high court judge.[6] The first activity I got involved with was an anti-war march to the war memorial on Armistice Day in 1933. It was celebrated afterwards because it was attacked by the boat clubs, and the boat clubs were routed, so that advertised the party and the membership grew quite considerably. Of course there were lots of political meetings going on because Hitler had just come to power and political issues were very much to the fore.

Apart from Cumming-Bruce, I don't think we ever had anybody else at Magdalene that belonged to the party but I do remember going to a meeting there on behalf of the British Union of Fascists. They had invited George Buchanan who was an ILP member; he was speaking on behalf of the Fascists and I went there to see what was going on, as it were. My recollection is that they held the tiniest meeting, not many people turned up. However, they were doing their best to get a foothold in Cambridge, and there was one time when Mosley came to Sawston about twelve miles away. In Cambridge at that time there was a Labour Club and a Socialist Club and the Socialist Club was mostly party members and much bigger than the Labour Club, and we decided that we would go and deal with this meeting of Mosley. We all biked out in the evening and practically filled the hall, and then as they got started with the meeting, people got up and walked out quietly, one after the other, until the audience dwindled to virtually nil. Then we had to bike back to Cambridge and I think in those days you had to get in by 10 o'clock, so there was a series of fines for being late. But it was quite successful in dealing with the Blackshirts.[7]

Along with all the other communist parties in the world, the basic party organisation at Cambridge was the cell: in my case that would be St John's and Magdalene. That would meet together regularly and every so often there would be an aggregate at which the general issues were discussed. There were students at Cambridge from lower middle-class backgrounds but I think I was pretty much alone in being somebody whose father was unemployed. Trinity and King's were where the party was strong. I did learn at one time that this chap Guy Burgess had joined the party. He had an accent that was upper, upper class; it rather got on my nerves, and he always had a languid attitude to everything which also didn't fit with me. When he graduated from the university, I heard that he was working for the Conservative Central Office and I remember saying, 'That's just what I thought that bastard would do'. I've always felt that I owed him an apology.

We took very seriously the question of the impact of Marxism upon what we were studying. There had been college mathematical societies which listened to mathematical theorems and puzzles and that sort of thing, but we formed a body called the Archimedeans, on the grounds that Archimedes was an applied mathematician as well as a brilliant mathematician as such. I was essentially the founder of that. This was partly because of the influence of G. H. Hardy, who published a book early in the war called *A Mathematician's Apology*, whose argument was that the one thing you can say about pure mathematics is that it never does anybody any harm. He used to have a picture of Lenin hanging in his study but that wasn't advertised: you had to go into his study to see that. He was an ultra-pure mathematician, and the idea of the Archimedeans was that this was a narrow view and that we should accept and indeed propagate the notion that mathematics can be useful. Of course, there was a lot of graduate unemployment in the middle thirties and one of the things we did was to run a survey of the jobs that people went into when they graduated. At that time something like ninety per cent went on to be school teachers, so they trained in higher mathematics in order to go and teach lower mathematics in schools and very little else. The society was just people who were interested, though I think one or two of them were party members. It rapidly grew to be the largest mathematical society and when I went to Cambridge in the sixties, the Archimedeans was the mathematical society.

We were very much encouraged by the party to work hard at our studies. I remember Pollitt coming down and saying that for third-year people your main job was to get a first. I had just started as a graduate student when the Spanish War started and there was a heavy involvement. John Cornford and a very famous mathematician named Colin McLaurin, the one that started McLaurin's bookshop, got killed in Spain. Cornford was by far the outstanding figure, he was the organiser and he was the man who brought down to us what the party line was on various issues. We were very disciplined, but if you had objections to what was said, this was taken seriously and it was explained to you why you were wrong. Nobody that I recall was ever expelled, because they were typically persuaded that they were wrong. Discipline is probably a misleading word because nobody was actually ever disciplined that I know of. Still, the attitude was that you were expected to do things and you were expected to agree with what the party nationally did, and if you didn't something was done to persuade you. There wasn't much, though: everybody, non-party as well as party people, was anti-fascist, and of course the party was anti-fascist, so these issues didn't really arise at that time.

James Klugmann was very prominent, and I also worked with Maurice Cornforth to try and set up communist groups in the countryside around Cambridge. We used to cycle out to Thaxted every Sunday morning and meet a chap who at the time was working on the roads; he was unemployed and wouldn't get his benefit unless he did that, and he had enquired about joining the Communist Party. We'd studied Marx on the theory of rent and went out to try and persuade people to attend to what we had to say rather than play dominoes, with almost no success at all: they were much more interested in their dominoes. We called once or twice on Conrad Noel, who had been appointed by the Countess of Warwick to be parson of Thaxted and had a curate named Jack Putterill who acquired a certain amount of notoriety because he led unemployed workers' marches at the time of the hunger marches.

The party members in the town were separate, and in fact there were very few members in the town itself. We did do our best to help them. There was a time when, for the first time ever, the busmen of Cambridge went on strike over pay and we ran meetings in the local labour hall to entertain and encourage the people on strike. Bejay, who used to write for the *Daily Worker*, had written a play about a strike, a comic thing making fun of the Marxist phrases and so on, and we put that on. I was one of the characters and that went down quite well with them and from then on I never paid my fare on the Cambridge bus. They would always say 'that's all right, sir'—that's the funny thing: 'that's all right, sir'. University students stood out and they were normally addressed as 'sir' by busmen at that time.

After postgraduate study at Princeton University, George Barnard returned to Britain in 1939 and began his lecturing career at Imperial College. He eventually became Professor of Mathematics at the University of Essex. He left the CPGB in the 1950s: 'what finished me was the six Jewish doctors'.

Ralph Russell
St John's College, 1937–40

I was born in 1918 in Homerton, where my father was the master of a work-house. That was quite an important and well paid job, but my father was a great spendthrift and did what a number of spendthrifts do, he put his hand in the till, hoping to pay it back before the reckoning day came, and got caught out. He was dismissed, and my mother, who was matron in the work-house, was dismissed with him. I was too young to have more than the vaguest recollections of what life there had been like, so I was never aware that we descended from a fairly affluent mode of life to a sort of genteel poverty. Eventually my father found a job, or was found a job which he felt obliged to take, and worked for the Board of Guardians in St George's in the East, which later came under the LCC. That was in 1925 and we moved to Loughton in Essex in 1925 where we attended the ordinary elementary council schools. Then at the age of ten I won a scholarship to what was prop-erly called Chigwell Grammar School, which was a minor public school. I was there from 1928 to 1937, when I won a scholarship to go to Cambridge.

I think that the fact that I grew up in a school with working-class chil-dren up to the age of ten really did something to influence my subsequent outlook on life, because when I went to the grammar school, to Chigwell school, I found that we were regarded by the toffee-nosed types with fee-paying parents as a very inferior lot who couldn't talk properly. I resented that very much. I thought: here's these bloody people, a lot of clots, I'm much cleverer than they are, who the hell are they to despise me? I always felt that.

My parents were what you'd call non-political, which meant inert Tories, of course. Formally speaking they were Church of England. My father was-n't in the least interested in religion anyway. My mother was fairly irreverent about religious things, but more generally religious than my father and quite commonly went to church. A very remarkable change came over in her out-look when the Spanish Civil War broke out. She was passionately in favour of the Spanish republican government and furious with the British gov-ernment for its policy of so-called non-intervention. Up to that she'd not shown any interest whatever in politics, but she really engaged in that issue and wrote to our Tory MP, who was extremely indignant that one of his serfs would take attitudes of this kind.

What first began to turn me in the direction of politics was what I can only describe as a great spiritual crisis of a kind which I simply can't analyse. This happened in 1933 or early 1934. I got absolutely suicidal and felt that I'd lost religion and that I hadn't got any guide to how I should conduct my life, and that I felt absolutely desperate about this, until I sort of decided, again more or less suddenly, that what I needed as a guide to life was what nowadays would be called humanism. One of the early consequences of this was that I became a pacifist. By the late twenties a general awareness of what a beastly business the whole First World War had been was spreading, and one of the indicators of that is that when *All Quiet on the Western Front* was published in March 1929, it was immediately translated into English and in the edition I've got there are three reprints in the month of April alone. People were much exercised at that time by the thought; good God, the war's only ended in 1918, it looks like another one is looming up, what can we do to stop it? We'd no idea of what it would be all about or anything like that, but we didn't want another war and we had some idea of how terrible the last war had been and how revolting were the hypocritical and lying attitudes of the people on all sides who waged the war, and the suffering of thousands and thousands and thousands of people because of the way in which these buggers carried on.

So I decided that the logical thing to do was to be a pacifist and under no circumstances ever to take part in any war. I was much influenced by a book called *The Psalms for Modern Life* illustrated by a man called Arthur Wragg with an introduction by Dick Sheppard, who was a very well known pacifist. This first brought me into a clash with the school authorities because in that kind of school in those days it was assumed that you would join the Officers' Training Corps, which the communists used to call with considerable justification the British equivalent of the Hitler Youth. When you reached the age of sixteen you were called together by the master who was in charge of the OTC and I put up my hand and said: I'm not going to join. There was a great kerfuffle about this and I had to go and see the school chaplain but in the end they let it pass. Later, after I joined the party, I took in some literature of the British Anti-War Movement to sell. One of the things they published was a book of photographs showing photographs of people who had been terribly mutilated in the First World War, to shock people. My headmaster was absolutely outraged; and told me I must collect in all the literature that I'd distributed and not bring such things to the school, even for my own reading

At about that time, my elder brother got to know a boy whose father was a convinced socialist. Through this boy, and ultimately his father too, we felt sympathetically inclined towards socialism; and I remember going to a street-corner meeting in Woodford, where a man called Nat Whine, who later became a full-time Labour Party functionary, was arguing that the cause of war in these days was capitalism. I was convinced by his argument and joined the Labour League of Youth early in 1934. At that time the proscription against communists had already long been in force and quite a number of the party members, in my opinion quite justifiably, concealed the fact that they were party members in order to join the Labour Party organisations. One was a chap in our local branch in Woodford called George Miles. Everybody knew he was a communist and nobody raised questions of expelling him, although they knew he wasn't supposed to be in it. I remember being extremely puzzled by the fact that nobody in the Labour League of Youth seemed to pay any attention to the major current political issues of the day at all. With the danger of war approaching, you'd have thought that they would at any rate think about what the Labour Party did at the time of the First World War and reach some conclusion about it, but they weren't interested. Well George Miles was interested, and George Miles carried on the argument that capitalism was the cause of wars to say that if capitalism is the cause of war, how do we get rid of capitalism? They hadn't any idea of how to get rid of capitalism. He convinced me and I became a communist, though I was kept waiting to join the party. I took part in the big anti-fascist demonstration of September 9th 1934, which remains the biggest and most impressive demonstration I've ever taken part in. In the end I was admitted to the party in December 1934.

Two things I remember. First, we used to meet and read together, first, the *Communist Manifesto*, and then the *Programme of the Communist International*. We would take it in turns to read paragraph by paragraph and at the end of each paragraph we would halt and discuss what we'd read. The main practical activity I remember was selling the *Daily Worker* and also the paper of the Busmen's Rank and File Movement, the *Busman's Punch*, which I used to sell outside the bus terminus in Loughton. I also remember being sent to Epping, which was miles away, to do the same thing, and I did all this without question. George Miles instilled in me that your whole life should be dominated by what served the interests of communism, and if there are things which it's your duty to do and you don't like doing them, well, tough, mate: you've got to do it because you're a communist. I did lots of things that I didn't like doing because I thought it was my communist duty to do so. The other thing I remember is that he used to quote a thing from one of the early documents of the party where it said, 'In the Communist Party there is no rank and file'.[8] He meant that every communist must be a leader, and you don't wait for what the leaders say, you work out what you've got to do and you do it; which again I think is a very valuable principle, though one which the communist parties and the whole Comintern abandoned years and years and years ago.

I was always very good academically and usually came up first in all the subjects at school. I loved Latin and Greek, which were the headmaster's speciality and which occupied a totally disproportionate part of the school syllabus, but I liked it and I was good at it. It was always assumed that people at our school who did well enough would go to Cambridge, and though I didn't win a major scholarship, I did win a scholarship and went to Cambridge to study classics in 1937.

The people in the Cambridge branch knew that I was coming, because there'd been a bloke there called George Barnard who had finished at Cambridge in the summer of the year before I went up, and he knew George Miles. One thing that annoyed me was snobbishness on the part of the ex-grammar school, ex-public school people in the party, because I didn't know how to behave as well-educated people behaved. I was much repelled by the sort of upper-class attitudes of most of the Cambridge communist students and felt extremely miserable there in the atmosphere. I hated the bloody Cambridge atmosphere anyway, the snobbishness and the assumption that Cambridge mortals are superior to other mortals just because they're at Cambridge. Then I met a chap called Bob Hone, who was in the party in my college, senior to me, and who was a genuine proletarian. His father was a militant bricklayer and I became friendly with him and he more or less saved my life spiritually speaking. I remember Bob saying at an aggregate meeting once, 'The comrades here, they lead double lives. In politics they're communists, the rest of their lives they're not communists at all.' This was greeted with superior laughter, but it was absolutely true. Ram Nahum read a kindly lecture to me, saying, 'Look, these people can't help their class background any more than you can help yours, and you can try and be a bit understanding and realise that you've got to work together'. We then did that and I went on to the leadership of the party in my second year and probably became the leading bloke in the Cambridge party.

The student population at the time was about five thousand. The town branch was entirely separate, and not only that, the students were separately organised from the staff. I thought this was absolutely absurd, that you should have separate university branches and never the bloody twain shall meet. Of the five thousand students, a thousand were members of the Cambridge University Socialist Club, which was under our leadership, as at that time the Labour Party bureaucracy for some reason didn't prohibit communists joining their student organisations. We must have had a party branch of something like two hundred by the time I left Cambridge in 1940, the whole atmosphere in those times was one very favourable to us, which I may say wasn't seriously affected by the outbreak of the war, despite the fact that the party under Comintern instructions then declared that it was an imperialist war. I was due for call-up before the war broke out, but students who were beginning their final year were allowed to take their degree before they were called up. So I did that, and I was called up within days of the fall in France.

After serving in India during the war, Ralph Russell became a lecturer and eventually professor in Urdu at the School of Oriental and African Studies at the University of London. He remained a member of the CPGB until its dissolution in 1991. He recently published a first volume of memoirs: Findings, Keepings. Life, Communism and Everything *(London, 2001).*

John Maynard Smith
Trinity College, 1938–41

From the age of eight to eighteen, I was at boarding school; from age thirteen at Eton. I hated it, essentially, I think, because I failed to become an accepted part of the social setup. I find this puzzling, because I have never failed to be accepted by any social group since—even working-class Coventry during the war, despite my upper-class accent. Perhaps because of this social exclusion, I came to loathe their snobbish and anti-intellectual attitudes and the rituals and clothes used to reinforce them: if you want to prevent a boy from fraternising with the working classes, make him wear a top hat. To be fair, I must add that they taught me mathematics with great skill—I have been exploiting what they taught me ever since. Politically, I left Eton a committed pacifist. A major reason for this was that both my parents had been in France during the first war, and passed on to me a conviction that war is the worst thing that can happen. I later found that several of my contemporaries had embraced pacifism for similar reasons.

Before leaving Eton and going to Cambridge, I spent a month in Berlin staying with my uncle, Noel Mason Macfarlane, who was British military attache there. My pacifism did not survive the visit—I returned from Germany convinced that Hitler had to be stopped, and that he would not be stopped by pacifist methods. Otherwise, I was a complete political ignoramus. My arrival in Cambridge coincided with the Munich settlement. Almost my first act was to join the socialist club (CUSC), which at that time had, I think, 1,000 members. All its officers were members of the Communist Party, and its policies were those of the party. My own few political convictions coincided with those of the party—a dislike of the British class system, a conviction that Hitler must be resisted, and a rather ill-formulated belief that the colonies must be given independence.

It soon became obvious to me that the activities of CUSC were directed by the party. The party members I came to know were far better informed than I was, and the party was a very effective organisation. I came to think that, if one wanted to be politically effective, one must join the party. I did so after one term at Cambridge, at Christmas 1938. When I joined I thought of Stalin as a dictator: admiration for the Soviet Union played no part in my decision. These deviationist views soon came to the attention of my new colleagues, and I was instructed to attend a training course on communist policy, Marxist philosophy and Soviet history in the vacation. The close link between the philosophy of dialectical materialism and practical politics was typical of communist thinking, and I fully accepted it.

During my first year at Cambridge, the party was on a roll, and its policy of resistance to Hitler increasingly popular. There was little formal opposition: what there was came from the college sports clubs—rowing and rugby. But things got tougher in 1939–40. In August we were shattered by the news of the Soviet-German non-aggression pact. My own attitude was that the Russian communists were so much wiser and better informed than I was that they had to be right. But when war was declared in September, the British party opposed the war as an imperialist war. I found this harder to excuse: I defended the policy out of loyalty, but I don't think I ever really accepted it. After these two events, a political opposition to the party rose in the social-ist movement in Cambridge, led by students loyal to the Labour Party. For the communist party this was a year of rearguard action, defending our lead-ing role in CUSC. During my final year at Cambridge Russia was now our ally and things were easier.

What of the Gulags? The short answer is that I did not believe reports of Soviet oppression: in common with many in the British party, I dismissed them as capitalist propaganda. I find it interesting to compare my attitude, which I think was shared by many contemporaries, with that described in their autobiographies by Doris Lessing and Eric Hobsbawm. They both had personal knowledge of what was happening in Europe, and had a more cyn-ical, and accurate, picture of the party. Yet they remained loyal to the communist cause. I think that one reason for my continuing loyalty, and per-haps for theirs, was that it is hard to leave a sinking ship: almost all my friends were in the party, and we were in it together.

After working in aircraft design, John Maynard Smith took a second undergraduate degree in biology after the war and became a lecturer and subsequently professor of biol-ogy, finishing his career at the University of Sussex. He ceased to be politically active in 1946 and was first disillusioned in communism by the Lysenko affair. He left the CPGB in 1956.

Cyril Claydon
Magdalene College, 1939–42

I was born in 1920 in Shoeburyness, Essex, a miserable dump of a place. My mother was a teacher, although she wasn't allowed to teach full-time when she was married. My father was a clerk on the railway and apart from the Great War he worked on the railway from the age of fourteen right until he retired at the age of sixty-five. He wasn't particularly socialist, but he was a strong trade unionist and one of my first memories is being taken by him to a strike meeting in 1926. Because my father was a trade unionist and a member of the Railway Clerks' Association he was persuaded by a colleague to take the *Daily Herald* when it was relaunched by the TUC as a popular paper, I think it was in 1930. Therefore I read the *Herald* and by the age of thirteen I became really interested in politics. I remember reading a series of articles, I think they were by Hannen Swaffer, about the terrible conditions that people lived in the slums and the big cities. Then I was alarmed by the rise of fascism, I was very thoughtful about things like that.

I had got a scholarship to the Southend High School for boys. At first they tried to exclude me because of my appearance—I was born without an ear and my jaw was wonky. Growing up like that made me shy; probably turned in on myself and made me more of a studious person than an active person. At the age of thirteen and a half I started to borrow political books from library, a very unnatural child: Engels's, *Socialism: Utopian and Scientific*, and then during my teens I read Sidney and Beatrice Webb's book on *Soviet Communism* and a book on *Dialectics* by Tommy Jackson. I was also shocked by the amount of poverty there was. We were sort of lower middle-class, not too badly off, not too well off; but my mother's family lived in London and I used to travel up to London and see the conditions in the East End and think, well, how ridiculous, you know; all this poverty and unemployment, and yet with modern science one should be able to create a good life for everybody. So that convinced me that I should become a socialist.

That's how I joined the Labour League of Youth in Southend. This used to meet in a funny old room on top of an old building which was called a mangle hospital, they sold and repaired mangles. It was an interesting experience because there were all sorts of leftists, all sorts of socialists, anarchists, people who were supporters of the CP in the Labour League of Youth. There wasn't a YCL in Southend in those days, so I stayed in the Labour League of Youth from 1934 to 1939. There was a good size Communist Party in Southend, about fifty members, and a group of us used to meet in secret as a communist faction within the Labour League of Youth. When the right wingers got wind of it, they just bolted out and left us in charge. I was a party sympathiser: I got on very well with them and accompanied CP members to London on one occasion to take part in one of the Hunger Marches. But my parents were against me joining so I couldn't very well while I was living at home.

Cambridge was a bit of a culture shock. In 1939 I went up to study modern languages on an exhibition, or minor scholarship, and that took me to Magdalene College: not the happiest choice because it was a terribly exclusive college. Nearly everybody there came from either Eton or Charterhouse and they all had these awful upper-class accents. With my outlook, I hated them, which wasn't a good start really. But I quickly got in touch with the party, so really all my life there was the party—either the Communist Party or the Socialist Club. I didn't have much to do with these upper-class types.

In the party there was an over-idealistic academic attitude, a sort of removal from reality in a sense, so that when I left Cambridge it was another terrible culture shock. Because it was an artificial life. We were living in these colleges and despite the war had nice dinners in the evening—lovely dinners in the college hall. So it was an artificial life but at the same time a very political life. I worked quite well the first year and got a First in part one, but after that I got more and more immersed in the work of the party and my third year there I was branch secretary of the student branch and I did very little academic work. I thought, well, I'll catch up in the third term, but there was too much so I got a bad degree as a result, a 2:2. I remember people saying that a communist student should be a good student. We paid lip-service to that and didn't do it, or at least I didn't. Ralph Russell set a bad example, he didn't do any academic work, but he later went back to study: a very dynamic and capable person he was, a very good speaker; he was the secretary the first year. The secretary the second year was John Maynard Smith. He was a very brilliant person studying engineering. Raymond Williams was in the CP too, but he was very laid-back; he didn't do much.

There was a lot of friction between the town branch and the students: generational friction. There were also the dons, and once a month I used to meet the secretary or representative of the lecturers' branch, which was Maurice Dobb; I used to go to his house, have a cup of coffee and a cigarette with him and have a little chat. Otherwise there was not a lot of interaction between the branches. One funny thing is that in the third year I was there the Soviet Union had come into the war and there was a tremendous upsurge among working people in favour of the Soviet Union and a lot of people joined the CP, but somehow that didn't happen in Cambridge. I don't know why but it went in the opposite direction and the party was smaller that year than the previous year.

After working for the YCL, the CPGB and the Daily Worker, *Cyril Claydon became a journalist on local newspapers in Kent and Sussex. He remained a member of the CPGB until 1991 when he joined the Democratic Left.*

Norman Lindop
Queen Mary College, London, 1940–2

I was born an only child in Reddish, Stockport in 1921. My father was an engineering draughtsman and my mother had worked for ten years in a cotton mill. My father's father was a boilermaker and worked at Gorton Tank, where Harry Pollitt had been. My father was always left-wing, and even before they were married he was a member of the ILP and refused military service in the First World War, on political grounds.

He was discontented with the job he had at Trafford Park and in 1929 he got a job in Ipswich. In Stockport he'd always taken a prominent ILP or Labour line at work and been a member of the union, and at first when he moved down to Ipswich he did the same thing. However, gradually he secured promotion and found it more and more embarrassing to be a trade union activist on the one hand and someone who was obviously regarded as future management on the other hand. Even so, he was active during the thirties in the trades and labour council and the Labour Party. I remember his fury with MacDonald when he deserted the Labour government, and he was active in the Peace Ballot carried out on behalf the League of Nations Union in the mid-1930s. What inspired his politics I don't know. I do know he was inspired by the Russian revolution, and he remained a Trotskyist in a way from that time on. Trotsky impressed him as an intellectual, and he despised Stalin before we knew anything about Stalin as a despot. Even in the glory days of the war he would never give on the question of the Soviet Union, because he blamed Stalin for what happened to Trotsky, quite correctly. You would never have thought to see my father, and to realise the positions he held in industry by that time, that he had this strong personal feeling for Trotsky—because I never met anyone else who had, really! He also didn't entirely trust Lenin, oddly enough; he thought him a short-term tactician and he was all for grand principles and sticking by them. One thing I regret is that I didn't give him sufficient credit for his opinions, and we had a lot of rows.

So I was brought up with a way of looking at the world from the point of view of the Labour Party. When my parents married they lived for a time in my grandfather's house and I can remember there being heated political discussions. Even my grandfather, who was a Liberal, felt sufficiently strongly to argue with my father about it on a daily basis. My mother shared my father's outlook but she was let down by her lack of education and wasn't a very articulate person. She instinctively empathised with Labour causes and would work her socks off in the committee room, stuffing envelopes and helping at election time, but she wouldn't be able to say very much about policy. She had gone through a Salvation Army phase apparently, but both my parents were very firmly anti-religious by the time I was conscious and that had a strong influence on me. They weren't married in church and I had to organise humanist funerals for them both.

When we moved to Ipswich in 1929, this was in the days when northern industrial towns had a continuous pall of smoke over them, and we realised when he got to Ipswich that we'd never really seen the sun. That was the biggest single change: seeing the sun and getting sunburnt in the ordinary course of events. I remember the first Christmas we were there and our families came down on the train, seeing them coming towards the barrier and thinking how pale they looked. I went to the local primary school and I was the only boy in my class of forty who got through to the secondary school. There was one other boy who qualified but his parents couldn't undertake to keep him at school until sixteen. I never saw those boys again: it's extraordinary what a social divide that constituted, though that was compounded by the fact that the school I went to was a new school built on the outskirts of Ipswich, so my parents sold their house and moved nearer the school.

Nowadays the school would be classified as a secondary-technical. When I left I didn't get a state scholarship and my father was quite content that I should go into the civil service.[10] Then when war broke out they cancelled all the civil service exams for the duration, so I got a job as a lab assistant and enrolled for a correspondence course to prepare for an external London degree. However, my mother decided that this wasn't good enough: all the other five in my year at sixth form had gone off to higher education and so why shouldn't I go? The first reason was that I'd got no money, so she went and almost camped out on the education department doorstep in Ipswich, until they gave in and gave me a major award. It was £54 plus fees: still nowhere near enough for a year, so my father took out a loan and began giving evening classes. I applied to do chemistry and was offered a place by Queen Mary College, which was in Cambridge. QMC was offered hospitality by King's College so I spent two and a half years in King's. I never quite got out of the cultural shock as a suburban, backwoods boy from quite modest surroundings, and the atmosphere which still prevailed during the war of an elitist kind of amateur approach to life.

So I would never have had this experience if it hadn't been for the war. The nucleus of the male QMC students who were living in King's included some politically active people, including three or four communists, the first I had consciously met. Like everybody else, I had been bitterly disappointed by the outcome of the Spanish Civil War. One of the masters from my school was Lon Elliott, who had gone in the International Brigade and been wounded and come back. That impressed me at the time, and it's impossible now to reconstruct the emotional impact of the defeat of the Spanish government on people like me, made all the worse by the fact that it seemed to have been facilitated by the appeasement by the west. The other thing that I was conscious of in Cambridge was the tradition of political activity. What typified that was John Cornford, the poet who was killed in Spain, who was a very potent symbol for people of my generation. When his poems and letters home were published as a book with him on the cover that was a very powerful sort of image.[9]

The other thing that happened at Cambridge was that the National Union of Students evacuated to Cambridge. In my last year at QMC I was president of the college union, and went to the NUS council meetings and that was how I got to know Margot Gale (later Kettle), the NUS secretary. Brian Simon was by then in the army, but he and Margot had saved the NUS in 1940 when there was a considerable movement to close the universities as being inappropriate and wasteful of manpower during an emergency.

I can remember how impressed I was by Margot, who was very moderate and reasonable and hardly ever raised her voice. Some people like Brian were obviously known as communists. Later I began to realise that Margot also was probably a communist, but it wasn't a big issue then. In any case, if you were going to be politically active, who did you belong to? There was a rather feeble Labour organisation, the National Association of Labour Student Organisations, but Labour always had trouble with its youth and student movement and it didn't seem to be doing anything, it only seemed to be the communists who were doing anything. I wasn't completely happy with the communist line in 1940 and early 1941, and the People's Convention seemed to be deliberately evading the issue of the war because of the Molotov-Ribbentrop pact. Then came the Soviet entry into the war, and from that time on it was all glory and that was fine.

I don't know when I joined the Communist Party. I sometimes wonder if I ever did, because they may have preferred me to remain as a sleeper and I was never a very active communist. I never sold a copy of the *Daily Worker* and I didn't publicise the fact; I didn't deliberately conceal it, but on the other hand I didn't publicise it. My activities were all in the student and later on in the youth movement, very broad-based, and I never became involved in political activity of a party nature. Also I never regarded myself as having been at Cambridge and was very proud of being a London student. I don't think communists much stood except for their political outlook. The party line was that you were supposed to be good students and I managed to get a First.

Afterwards I felt let down, and still do but I've never felt betrayed in any vital way. I went into it with my eyes open, and took risks in the sense of believing things on very little evidence and I shouldn't have done that. But we were all wet behind the ears.

After working part-time for the World Youth Congress, Norman Lindop began his academic career at Queen Mary College in 1946 and was eventually Director of Hatfield Polytechinc, now the University of Hertfordshire. He was knighted in 1973.

Dorothy Wedderburn (Barnard)
Girton College, 1943–6

I was born in Walthamstow, East London, September 1925. My father was a cabinet maker and my mother had left school at thirteen in Norfolk and gone into domestic service. They had a daughter and a son fairly close together, and then the daughter died of rheumatic fever and I was born as a sort of replacement; so I had one brother, George, who was ten years older than I was. My mother had very little education but she was extremely alert and bright. My father also was an extremely intelligent man who had missed out an education in the sense that he'd got a place at the local grammar school, but hadn't taken it up because his mother was a widow with eight or nine children. Therefore he was apprenticed instead and became a very dedicated trade unionist. He wasn't particularly politically active, though they both always voted Labour and in any discussion he was always on the left. But he was a very strong trade unionist and I understand that he always refused promotion to foreman because he didn't want to leave the ranks. As I was growing up he experienced unemployment two or three times, and I can remember him coming home with his tools and my mother sort of distressed: 'You haven't lost your job again?'. So there was never very much money, and quite a lot of anxiety at those times; but he was never out of work more than six months or a year.

My brother got a scholarship to the local grammar school and became very politically involved and joined the YCL. Of course he had a tremendous influence on me. At Cambridge he was a contemporary of John Cornford's and the sort of the thing I grew up with as a young person was a photograph of John standing on our bookshelves which he'd put there. George became secretary of the undergraduate branch of the Communist Party, and as far as I can make out spent a lot of his time travelling up to London doing political organising, but didn't himself go to Spain. That's another of my early memories: going to a *Daily Worker* bazaar with George, while he discussed whether or not he should go to Spain and me thinking, 'I don't want him to go to Spain, I don't want him to be killed'. With great encouragement from all the young YCL people that I got to know through him, I was instrumental in setting up something which had the incredible title of Schoolboys' United Front. It actually had three girls in it, but it was still called Schoolboys' United Front! It had no political affiliation but discussed things like the growth of fascism and what was happening in Spain. George also took me along to political meetings, and my father did too: I remember I heard Tom Mann speak when I was very young. Either just before the war or after the war, my parents did eventually join the Labour Party, though my mother was the one who got rather more involved. Of course we always went on May Day marches and I also had a very secular upbringing. My mother had gone into domestic service when she came to London with a clergyman and she developed an enduring hatred of the Church of England as a result of that. They didn't stop me going to Sunday School, but very early on I was convinced that there was no such thing as God.

Walthamstow was a very good Labour local authority. It's got some buildings which my father was involved in building, like Walthamstow town hall, which are rather reminiscent of Soviet architecture. It also had a very good educational system which was very supportive. I went to the local elementary school and then I got a scholarship to Walthamstow High School for Girls, which was evacuated to Wellingborough during the war and shared premises with Wellingborough Girls School. There was quite a lot of argument about my going to university. My mother was very much opposed to me going and said, 'All she'll do is get married'. My father, however, was very supportive, which is unusual in terms of the sociological literature. He very much was the one who felt that he would have gone if he'd had the chance and it was a wonderful opportunity: the fact that I was a girl shouldn't stop me from doing it.

So I went up to Cambridge in October 1943. I hated going up for the interview to Girton: I can remember being absolutely terrified by these hordes, as it seemed to me, of huge Cheltenham Ladies' College and Roedean girls, roaming the corridors, knowing everybody and having introductions to all the dons. I remember making friends with one other girl who seemed working class, and the two of us sitting there in our rooms, trying to get a fire going and feeling very terrified. I have terribly ambivalent feelings about Cambridge, and it was really my experience at Girton that I found so unsatisfactory. There were awfully few people with my sort of background there and we gravitated together a bit, but so many of these young women had been at boarding school and that gave them a degree of self-assurance. So most of my life centred outside, in the university. It was a very strange time in my first year because there were very few men around. Practically everybody was called up, and so one found oneself becoming secretary of everything, from the economics society, the Marshall Society, to the secretary of the party branch—which is what I ended up as.

By the time I went to Cambridge I was already quite sure that I wanted to join the Communist Party, though a year or two earlier I'd had a terrific argument with my brother about the Russians invading Finland. Compared to Girton, the party was much more relaxed and that's why I think I immersed myself in that. People I met through the party and through politics, like June Bean and Dorothy and Edward Thompson, were very much more congenial. By 1944, the end of my first year, there were also a few ex-servicemen returning.

We were lucky as economists because Maurice Dobb was teaching there. However, there were all sorts of problems: I mean, did you or did you not write your essays about the marginal theory of value, or did you try to introduce Marxist analysis? That was difficult, and as far as I was concerned in the end I copped out and I just regurgitated what I saw as the official Cambridge line. But it was a very much broader economic syllabus than it would be now: there was a lot of economic history and not quite so much emphasis on the theory. I was never supervised by Maurice but I was supervised by Joan Robinson, who was a strong Keynesian at that point; so there were tensions that people tried to explore. Joan Robinson and Nicky Kaldor were the charismatic people in the Economics faculty. Maurice was very much the outsider. I think his experiences had made him rather cautious, though in some ways he was absolutely wonderful and used to sell the *Daily Worker* if we asked him to, although he hated it. But he was certainly not a charismatic figure.

The party was very much a disciplined organisation. There were the generalised expectations which I could sum up by saying, 'Harry expects you to be a good student'. Maybe I've got an over-developed super-ego, but there was also the expectation that if you undertook to do things you had to do them. There was a national student organisation of the party which I got involved with in my last year. By then I had met my first husband, Max Cole, who even though he was a member of the party volunteered to go as a Bevin boy because he had a certain Quaker streak in him. Anyway Bevin Boys were given a great deal of weight in terms of national service, so he was working down the mines and there was a chance for him to get away and the question arose whether we should meet in London, as there was also a national meeting of some kind that I should have been going to. I didn't go to the national meeting, I went to meet Max instead, and I can remember being disciplined: interviewed by the national organiser and asked, 'Why weren't you there?'

Certainly, there wasn't very much bohemianism in that period. That was probably the effect of the war, but also it may have been that the class composition of the party had changed a bit since earlier in the thirties—partly because it was easier for people to go to university through ex-service grants and things like that. Anyway, we certainly weren't a bohemian lot, in fact we were really rather staid: I remember spending my first long vacation reading volume one of *Capital*. To give you a flavour of what it was like, you had to do a little test before you'd be admitted to the party saying what you had read. I already knew that I was a socialist and that the world had to be changed and I just thought that joining the party was the way to do it.

After graduating in 1946 Dorothy Wedderburn worked for four years at the Board of Trade. Subsequently as Lecturer and Professor in Industrial Sociology at Imperial College she published several books on redundancy, new technology the old aged and the welfare state. She left the CPGB in 1956.

Peter Worsley
Emmanuel College 1943–4, 1946–8

I was born on Merseyside in Birkenhead which is a very poor, proletarian place, but moved rapidly to Wallasey which was the opposite: a genteel, middle-class part of the Wirral. My father was an auctioneer, had quite a decent business, and then became an estate agent. Merseyside being Merseyside, what was important was whether you were a Catholic or a Protestant. My father was a Catholic and my mother was a Protestant, but in those days a woman had to convert if she got married, so she did though it didn't mean a thing.

I used to go across the river to St Francis Xavier's College in Liverpool. The journey really got me down and I hated the Jesuits who ran the place. Sadistic swine, they were, very austere and I would say cruel. If you were five minutes late for school, they had an instrument made of whale bone, like a long, long shoehorn, and they hit you over the hand with it, and you'd be sentenced to be punished for five on the hand: very painful. On the other hand, if you did good work in class you would be given a thing called a red bill, which was made of a kind of parchment, and it had a value: five, ten, fifteen, depending on how good your work was. It was written in Latin of course. The theory was that if you were sentenced to be punished you could hand in a red bill and get it cancelled. As a kid I always thought that was utterly amoral, utterly disgusting, because if you were going to be punished for something you'd wrongly done, you should be punished. The idea of trading it in for benefits stored up in heaven! But the worst thing about the Jesuits, and this is the second degree of amorality, was that you never knew whether they would accept the red bill and let you off or not. It was total indeterminacy, a sort of Stalinoid thing. So I hated the Jesuits, and the education in confessional schools was lousy then. I think it alienated me more widely from Catholicism so I gave it up when I got to Cambridge and encountered all these exciting ideologies.

In any case, my mother insisted I was taken away from there and so I went to Wallasey Grammar School, which was wonderful: very liberal and they taught you things. A major cultural influence had been the Catholic-Protestant division. As a Catholic you were a bit of an outsider: when I was head boy, during assemblies the Jewish boys and the Catholic boys were put in a little room at the side; and we used to do our homework and tell dirty jokes until the doors would open and you'd be allowed to stand along the side of the hall, and listen to the rest of the business. And then with Wallasey and Birkenhead, there was also a class difference. I can remember being very moved by blind men, standing outside my father's sale room with little notices on them saying, 'Blinded at the Somme', and with their medals on. The class difference between proletarian Birkenhead and petty-bourgeois Wallasey was huge.

My own family's values were boring, respectable, middle-class, conventional. In those days a young man never carried a parcel in public. Can you believe this? You'd go to the shops and buy something and it would be wrapped up in brown paper and string, but you mustn't be seen carrying such a thing as a man: it was delivered at the house. That kind of respectability was awful, and I used to be sickened with these smug bastards, all the kind of people my family admired so much. However, I didn't rebel against my parents, who were very tolerant, and my Catholic father was a very nice man. But it produces a kind of diffuse alienation, a rejection of the orthodoxies of that milieu.

I can remember just beginning to explore politics. I read a book by G.D.H. Cole about socialism and tried to find out what it was, and nobody knew. We had a master at school who had a BSc (Econ) and introduced us to a lot of things, ideas and problems of an economic kind and a political kind. Then

I went up to Cambridge and found myself right in the middle of it, it was absolutely marvellous. I had got a junior scholarship to Emmanuel College and went up in about January 1942, which was the height of the Nazi-Soviet head-on collision. There was this tremendous ferment of politics and that's what shaped my politics, and most people at the time.

We were a force in Cambridge then, and there were very highly organised tactics for converting people, really quite Jesuitical. There were these things called 'Consulting with Lenin'. You get a couple or three party members who meet with a potential recruit, let them know what they're doing, and ask them about their difficulties about joining the party. I remember doing this on Parker's Piece in Cambridge with a couple of party members. Gradually they would try and erode away all your objections, at which point they would expect you to join—and most people did in those days. I remember holding out for a long time about the Russian invasion of Finland, and I never really changed my mind about that. But in the context of what was happening in Europe as a whole in those days, and the world as a whole, the Russo-Finnish war was something rather parochial, it wasn't all that important. Anyway, there was nothing else really, nothing that had any kind of ideological cohesion about it, or alternative excitement. The Cambridge University Socialist Club was a pretty dynamic thing and it really was a very exciting world, with people like Edward Thompson and Dorothy. The first thing I ever wrote was a review of *Gone With the Wind* for the CUSC bulletin. The next task I was given was to write a piece about the Allied landings in North Africa. You did anything in those days.

As for Cambridge, I loved it mostly and had a marvellous time. It was very exciting intellectually, not just politically. However, the whole structure and hierarchy in Cambridge was and still is pretty ludicrous; there was the college system and a terrible, gross elitism. The collective ethos was that there were people who were at Cambridge, and there was the rest of the world, and they were barbarians—not worth talking about. I was firstly in the English Department and I'd been brought up at Wallasey by a Leavisite. He was a wonderful teacher and a wonderful person so he brought me up a total Leavisite, and when I went to Cambridge the first thing I wanted to do was go to Leavis's lectures; and my tutor, H. S. Bennett, a very boring man, said, 'Oh, I wouldn't do that if I were you'. I was discouraged, and so was everybody else: when I got to Leavis's lectures there were about ten people, everybody had been told not to go. It was different after the war when we came back from the army; then Leavis had achieved credibility and you found a hundred or a hundred and fifty people.

You got a year at university before you were called up for the army. This is a measure of the elitism of Cambridge and Oxford, because you were privileged immensely by serving in the Officer Training Corps. At first after I took my examination, I went and worked in a factory, because that was our dream, favouring the proletarian. I went off and worked in Pye's radio factory in Cambridge, and they hated us, the workers, because all these enthusiastic left wingers came in and did about three times the productivity of the workforce, suggesting of course that they weren't working very hard. Then the call-up came and you were sent straight to Officers Training Corps: I was sent to Llandrindod Wells to become an artillery officer, anti-aircraft. There were guys there who'd spent years in the army, who'd got children and families, and here's a raw, young kid from Cambridge, never had any experience of the army, put side by side with them. When I was demobilised there was a similar scheme, again privileging the Cambridge graduates, or university graduates.

I went back to Cambridge with great trepidation. What I really wanted to do was sociology so I asked my senior tutor, who had a very fascist sort of mentality: E.W. Welbourne, a man of working-class origin who wrote the history of the Durham miners: it's the only thing he ever did write. He said: 'We don't have sociology in Cambridge! There's something called social anthropology, you can do that if you want.' In fact, that was what I really wanted and didn't dare ask. So I did anthropology, but it was terrible, a lot of old fuddy-duddies of the worst order.

After graduating in 1948, Peter Worsley spent two years as a language tutor at the Overseas Food Corporation before beginning his academic career in the Department of Anthropology at Manchester University in 1950. He left the Communist Party in 1956 and was an editorial board member of the New Reasoner, 1956–9.

Dorothy Thompson (Towers)
Girton College, 1945–7

Neither Edward nor I felt any particular privilege in being at Cambridge. Edward's father was an Oxford don and Edward had a good knowledge of the snobbishness and exclusiveness of the Oxbridge establishment. My own family were musical/theatrical. When I was about ten I asked my mother what class we belonged to and she said, 'Working class of course', and I never questioned this. In fact, I suppose we were lower middle-class—my grandfathers were a journeyman shoemaker and merchant navy officer/Thames waterman. I had a cousin who went to his father's college at Cambridge just before I went up. My parents were trained as musicians—they had both attended the Royal Academy of Music as full-time students for a time. My mother worked throughout her life as a teacher and accompanist, and gave occasional recitals. For some years she ran a small private school which I attended for about two years. My father gave up a possible career as a singer and opened a music shop which started with selling musical instruments, sheet music and records but later sold wireless and then television. We had television sets in the late 1930s. Two of my father's brothers and several other members of my family were on the music halls. I went to a state secondary school although my brothers went as day boys to Dulwich College which was a South London public school.

I went up to Girton after having been in the YCL and the CP for three years. My parents, although not joiners themselves, had always been left radicals and my brother had been in the Labour League of Youth and for a time the Peace Pledge Union, though his group left at the time of the Spanish Civil War. In 1939, shortly before the war was declared, he volunteered for the air force. I used to spend a lot of my free time in the evenings and at weekends helping in the YCL office in London where Ted Willis was chairman and Mick Bennett was secretary. Both had been kicked out of the army. Ted, particularly, was a very charismatic chap and I learnt a lot about the theatre in particular from him. Incidentally, when I was interviewed at Girton by Helen Cam she asked me what newspapers I read. I answered cautiously, '*The Times* and the *News Chronicle*', and she said, 'And the *Daily Worker*?' I agreed that I did read the *Worker* and she said she could tell that from my papers, and added, 'I am a socialist myself'. I met Val Walker who was then the national student organiser at the YCL office in London. She had at one time a proposal that I should do a special job for the CP at Cambridge but this would mean my going up as a presumed non-party student. I refused partly on some kind of principle but also because I had done a lot of recruiting and speaking in Bromley and had been active for a couple of years in the Council for Education in World Citizenship—or some title like that. Several of my fellow sixth-formers from this organisation joined the CP at Cambridge and so would know I was a communist. There were underground members in many student organisations, among them the beautiful national secretary of the NUS, Margot Gale (later Kettle). I was later offered the job of national organiser of the ULF (later the SLF), a post until then held by Claire Cassy (later Yuille and Rabstein). I said I thought the post should be advertised but Val said that they could not risk a non-party candidate being appointed. I don't think that either Claire or Pegotty Freeman who were the officers of the ULF and lived and worked in Cambridge ever made any secret of their party membership.

As students the main concerns of the CP members were, in my first two years, doing voluntary war work—a shift a week in Pye's in my case, for which I also prepared breakfast for student volunteers in the CUSC club room in Round Church Street, doing some public campaigns and meetings. I remember being very angry because the CP hadn't asked us to do anything about the Bengal famine and we organised a meeting and wrote letters to the press. I think this was when Vicky got sacked from the *Evening Standard* for his brilliant cartoon, but I may not be remembering exactly. I was college group secretary of CUSC, responsible for organising and recruiting in the colleges. We also ran a procession and a Guildhall meeting supporting the Beveridge Report which was heavily barracked by the student Tories. I don't remember doing much about the academic side of things in those days. Our hero figures were John Cornford and Ram Nahum. Freddie Lambert who had been seriously wounded by the bomb which killed Ram was around, and she remained a friend for the rest of our lives.

In my second period, 1945–7, we did work on syllabus reform, particularly agitating against the political thought courses which looked at the texts independently of the social context in which they were written. We also ran a socialist history seminar which most of the CP history students attended but not any of the graduates and fellows as I recall. We were particularly excited by Vico whose work was being published in English for the first time around then, and in the Leveller Tracts of which a collection came out about the same time. My contribution was a paper, my first academic presentation outside the tutorial system, on Linguet and *L'Esprit des Lois*—though I've probably got that title wrong as I haven't read it since then. It was awful.

The particular CP work that I did from 1945–7 was with the town branch. I lived for a time with Pearl and Sam Lilley and Pearl, who was a shop steward at Pye's, stood as communist candidate in the local elections and I acted as her agent. We did a lot of work on housing and other local questions and were helped by some of the staff CP members—I remember Maurice Dobb used to come out leafleting, and Frederick and Damris Parker-Rhodes and Priscilla and Nicholas Moor. Priscilla ran off with one of the comrades, an engine driver, I seem to recall.

Among the Cambridge people who went to Yugoslavia in 1947 to help build the Youth railway were Martin Eve, Steve Mason—who was by then a don and married to Bridget (later Hill) though she wasn't on the railway—and George (Sam) Sheperson, later Chair of Modern History at Edinburgh—a lifetime friend and solid man of the left. Essentially we were minor CP activists, not would-be academics or supporters of the academic establishment. We never concealed our CP membership or looked for jobs in the establishment, so wouldn't have been much use as spies. The one person in our lot who was approached by the Foreign Office in connection with the Yugoslav trip was at Oxford.

The Cambridge I remember carried on through people like the Cornfords, Christopher in particular; Sugden-Morris who became master of Trinity Hall was a man of the left and his wife Marian was in the CP as a student of Queen Mary College, which was evacuated to Cambridge in the war. David Holbrook is still there though he left the CP before 1956 I think. Dorothy Barnard stayed there for some time though she was a couple of years younger than I. Wolf Mankowitz, Malcolm Pine and Max Cole I had known while we were at school—not at the same one but in a schools organisation, and they all joined the student CP branch.

The main point I would make is that the CP was a formative element in the education of our generation, but not the only one. I don't think Edward or I ever felt any kind of bond with the university and never for one second thought of staying there to work. I suppose we considered universities, Oxbridge in particular, to be part of the structure of class domination in England. We both wanted to write and I wanted to write history. Edward saw himself as a freelance writer who increasingly wrote history books but whose first interest was always in literature especially poetry. His last finished book was on Blake.

We shared some interests but by no means all. For instance, having been on active service may have been at least as important as having been in the CP for some; participation in adult education both in the forces and in civvy life was formative. In the same way being in CP branches in which the non-educated were at least as bright and politically aware as the university blokes and blokesses inhibited academic hubris.

Dorothy Thompson was an active member of the CPGB Historians' Group until she left the party in 1956. She was later heavily involved in END. She taught at Rutgers in the USA and at the University of Birmingham. Her publications include The Chartists. Popular Politics in the Industrial Revolution *(1984) and* Outsiders. Class, Gender and Nation *(1993).*

June Bean
Newnham College 1943–5

I was born in Norwich in June 1924. My father was an engineering pat-ternmaker, which was a skilled job, but he lost his job in the slump in the 1930s so there was a considerable period of misery that impinged on me even at that young age. He felt ashamed of being unemployed; and my mother thought it was his fault, so it was horrible. My father was sort of a socialist, but he didn't talk about it very much, and he wasn't active in any-thing. He didn't belong to the Labour Party or any other party, and as far as I know he wasn't in a union, though he presumably had been earlier on. He did various ragbag jobs as I was growing up. One was that he was a tally-man—I think its proper name is credit drapery. These men go around with a little card full of samples, usually ladies' clothing, sometimes household linen, and they knock on doors and try to persuade people to buy them on tick. Then they create a round in an area and they go back weekly to collect a few shillings to pay off the debt. Before the debt is cleared they try and sell something else. It was really a bit beneath him to do that, and I don't expect he liked the social idea very much either, but he had a round in various parts of Norfolk. He'd been out of work for a couple of years and I suppose he couldn't get anything else.

My mother didn't work. She had been a shop assistant, but never worked after she was married. She wasn't an unintelligent person, but my father was very bright and she didn't involve herself in anything that involved any kind of discussion of ideas as she was afraid of exposing herself in front of him. During the war, because of his earlier training, my father was directed to war work inspecting crashed aeroplanes in Cambridge. My mother wanted to go and be with him, and I wanted to stay on at school because I was in the sixth form and didn't want to change, so they moved to Cambridge and I stayed in Norwich. I get left with a neighbour, which was freedom for me, because the neighbour was much younger, and my boyfriend was just down the road.

I had always been determined to be a doctor. All the teachers at my school tried to dissuade me. One of them said I was rising above my station, which only increased my determination. Initially, it was purely a sentimental thing. I had a favourite uncle who died a horrible death of cancer of the throat at home and I saw all this as a child of eight and, kid-like, I said: I'm going to put a stop to this, and tenaciously hung on to this idea that I was going to be a doctor and stop these nasty things happening. Of course, having embarked on this, and done sciences at school, nothing was going to stop me: I just got the bit between my teeth. I thought to be a doctor was a wonderful thing, to cure everybody and stop all this nastiness. Meeting opposition at school, when it got to deciding on subjects and applying for university, only confirmed me that this was what was I going to do. You couldn't study medicine in those days, you had to get a natural sciences degree and then apply for medical school. Therefore I did sciences for my higher school certificate, and of course we didn't have physics in a girls' grammar school, so I had to cycle across the city several times a week to the boys' school: one girl among several hundred boys! Of course I made relationships with the lads and one of them joined the Communist Party and so I kind of did too. This was 1943, which was the height of the popularity of the Soviet Union and the time when the party reached its maximum membership. I was conscious of what I was doing, but the move was not mine initially.

I wasn't very active in Norwich, probably because I was working too hard. When I got to Cambridge I hated it; or at least I hated it for the first year. I think probably the party was my salvation because I felt utterly out of my depth. I never met anybody in my immediate circle who had a working-class background and I found that was very difficult; I was a working-class kid who'd never mixed with people like this. I was really very miserable, so much so that, probably it was the first holidays, I went back to my old school and had a talk to the deputy head. What I said was that I didn't want to do medicine, rather than not stay at Cambridge. This was to do with the extremely upper-class lads—almost entirely lads—who were almost exclusively the sons of doctors, so that I think that the upper-classness of Cambridge was even more in evidence in the medical school than elsewhere. When we arrived, the head of the anatomy department made all the women—there were only about eight of us—stand to one side while the lads got the best seats. When that was done we could fit in the corners where best we could. I remember hearing him walking into the anatomy theatre with a visitor one day saying how he hated having women there, he hated their squawky, scratty voices. A nice atmosphere!

The atmosphere in the party branch was absolutely nothing like this. That was why it was a great help to me to cope with Cambridge, that I had this kind of normality in relationships within our party branch. Probably quite a lot of branch members did come from less privileged backgrounds, although it's a long time ago and I haven't a very detailed recollection. I was the student branch secretary for I suppose a couple of years. I don't remember anything about the people that had gone before, and we didn't have any contact with the adult university branch of the party either, not even me as secretary. Maurice Dobb was around at that time, and I knew a few names, but I never met them. The only contact we had with the town branch was during the 1945 election, and that was canvassing for the Labour candidate.

Mainly we were campaigning on broader issues, I don't remember student issues. I think it was really playing at politics and with hindsight it doesn't seem to me to have been terribly serious. There was a lot of talk and a few rambles in the country at weekends, we sat around in people's little college rooms and had a little discussion: but I don't recall us having much influence on anybody. I was political in the sense that I knew which side I was one, but I was never much of a Marxist scholar. I really wasn't a very political person at all except knowing which side I was on.

After going on to the West London medical school, June Bean worked in public health and finished her career at Newham Borough Council. She remained in the CPGB until

1991 and subsequently joined the Labour Party but resigned over the threatened imposition of charges for GP's consultations.

Notes

1. Eric Hobsbawm, *Interesting Times. A Twentieth-century Life* (London, 2002), p.119.
2. Stephen Woodhams, *History in the Making. Raymond Williams, Edward Thompson and Radical Intellectuals 1936–1956* (London, 2001), pp.23–33; see also Neal Wood, *Communism and British Intellectuals* (London, 1959).
3. Brian Harrison, 'Oxford and the Labour movement', *Twentieth-Century British History*, 2, 3, 1991, p.258.
4. The research was funded by ESRC award number R000 237924.
5. For a fuller recollection shortly after Cornford's death in Spain in December 1936, see Victor Kiernan, 'Recollections', in Pat Sloan (ed.), *John Cornford. A Memoir*, Jonathan Cape, 1938, pp.114–22.
6. Full name: A. R. Hovell-Thurlow-Cumming-Bruce. Victor Kiernan notes that this was 'one of the two brothers who were leaders when I was first taking part in the demonstrations. I remember asking the senior what distinguished communists from other socialists. His idea (not perhaps unmeaning) was that capitalism was doomed to collapse, and a strong CP would be needed to step in and prevent arnarchy. When they left it was rumoured that they had been tempted away from communism by the offer of a fishing holiday in Norway. I would be happier to believe that they had simply come to the end of their Cambridge spell, and were looking for a profession.'
7. Victor Kiernan adds: 'My own memory is of a Blackshirt meeting, somewhere in that direction, where our tactics were to shout them down. This was seen later to have been a mistake, which antagonised some neutral members of the audience. Perhaps this meeting was the result.'
8. See *Report on Organisation* presented to CPGB Sixth Congress (London, 1922), p.10.
9. See Sloan, *John Cornford.*
10. Norman Linsop adds: 'He was in any case firmly against my going into higher education, partly because of graduate unemployment in the 1930s.'

Paul Lafargue and
The Right to Be Lazy

David Renton

The purpose of this article is to consider the utopia of an often forgotten classic of the left, namely Paul Lafargue's pamphlet, *The Right to Be Lazy*. What is remarkable about this short book is its genre, which is both Marxist and utopian. For many good reasons, Karl Marx and Friedrich Engels avoided that sort of writing. In the 1840s, when they were first won to social-ism, the workers' movement suffered from a surfeit of utopian schemes. It was not that Marx or Engels had anything against utopias, *per se*. But think-ing of themselves as practical men, both were embarrassed by the disjunction between the glorious visions of William Weitling, Charles Fourier and Robert Owen among others, and the naivety with which they planned to get there. The results are scorned in Engels's *Anti-Dühring*,

> If pure reason and justice have not hitherto ruled the world, it is only because they have not been rightly understood. What was missing was only the individual man of genius, who has now arisen and who has recog-nised the truth. The fact that he has now arisen, that the truth has been recognised precisely at this moment, is not an inevitable event following of necessity in the chain of historical development, but a happy accident. He might just as well have been born 500 years earlier and he might then have spared humanity 500 years of error, strife and suffering.[1]

Engels's response to the utopian socialists was clear—no utopia mattered to him, unless its author knew which group in society was supposed to bring it into being. In this sense the Marxism of the founding fathers was very much a theory of the transition. What mattered to Karl Marx and Friedrich Engels was the task of describing the means of how to get to the new society, rather than the final end of what to do when they got there.

Similar tastes have been carried into the labour movement since. Marx hinted at the nature of the future communist society in passages from his

German Ideology and *The Civil War in France*.[2] Then, in the middle of the Russian revolution of 1917, Lenin considered the future of the state after a successful workers' uprising. His pamphlet, *The State and Revolution*, predicted that the revolution would abolish the coercive apparatus of the state. Without inequality there would be no class divisions, and without classes who would there be left to police?[3] In addition to this important example of utopian theory, scientific socialists have made do with a few short pamphlets, several Marxist utopias in the form of fiction, and...not much more than that.[4] We have no Marx 'On Socialism', no Engels, no Lenin, no Sartre, no Trotsky, no Serge.[5] The existing literature is not much of a guide when labour movement activists attempt to think of a post-capitalist society and perhaps this absence of discussion is one reason why so few socialists make the imaginative leap today.

The absence of utopian writing in the Marxist tradition helps to explain the appeal of Paul Lafargue's book. Certainly in the last two decades of the nineteenth century, his pamphlet was one of the three or four most popular books to be sold within the Second International. First published in summer 1880 as a series of articles in the newspaper *L'Égaliè* (Equality), *Le droit à la paresse* came out as a short book in 1881, with new editions following in 1883, 1898 and 1900. 'According to Alexandre Bracke, the longtime socialist deputy, it was the socialist pamphlet most extensively translated after the *Communist Manifesto* and was translated into Russian before the Manifesto.'[6] Charles Kerr of Chicago provided a first English translation based on the 1883 edition. Since then the pamphlet has continued in print, with the most recent French editions appearing in 1975 (Maspero) and 1994 (Mille et une Nuits), and English editions in 1989 (Charles Kerr) and 1999 (Fifth Season). *The Right to Be Lazy* was an important and widely read pamphlet, but Lafargue's has suffered as much as any of the socialist classics from the pessimism which has descended on the left since the fall of the Berlin Wall. For most of the past dozen years, there has been no English edition in print. Fifth Season must therefore be congratulated for their recent republication of *The Right to Be Lazy*, complete with a new translation by Len Bracken.[7]

In this article I will consider first, the life and career of Paul Lafargue; next, the argument of his pamphlet; then its source; and finally its reception since publication. One question is answered at the end of the article: how useful is Lafargue's pamphlet, how relevant is this utopia to labour movement activists, one hundred and twenty years after it was first produced?

A rebel life

Paul Lafargue was born in Santiago, Cuba, on 16 June 1842. Among his grandparents, Lafargue counted a French republican, a French Jew, a mulatto and a Caribbean Indian. In the words of the American syndicalist Daniel De Leon, 'Paul Lafargue had a constitutional affinity with the oppressed'.[8] Originally a supporter of the French socialist Pierre-Joseph Proudhon, Lafargue settled in London, and was acquainted with one of Proudhon's rivals within the First International, namely Karl Marx. Eventually won over to Marx's vision of socialism, Lafargue married the Old Moor's daughter Laura in 1865. Working as a political activist in Spain and France, Paul Lafargue helped to found the French Workers' Party, which was led by his friend Jules Guesde. He and his wife corresponded with Engels until his death in 1895. The loss of three children caused Laura and Paul to devote their lives solely to political work. Their partnership ended only in 1911, with their joint suicide.[9] Given that most socialists were suspicious of even voluntary euthanasia, it is appropriate to quote from Paul Lafargue's final note, which sets out his reason for ending his life in this way:

> Healthy in body and mind, I end my life before pitiless old age which has taken from me my pleasures and joys one after another; and which has been stripping me of my physical and mental powers, can paralyse my energy and break my will, making me a burden to myself and to others. For some years I had promised myself not to live beyond 70; and I fixed the exact year for my departure from life. I prepared the method for the execution of our resolution. It was a hypodermic of cyanide acid. I die with the supreme joy of knowing that at some future time, the cause will triumph to which I have been devoted for forty-five years. Long live Communism! Long Live the Second International.[10]

This short biographical summary highlights several of the themes which would matter in the genesis of *The Right to Be Lazy*, including Paul Lafargue's relationship with Karl Marx, the distinctive and unfinished character of his Marxism, and the relationship between the personal and the political, as it shaped Paul Lafargue's life.

Lafargue met Karl Marx at a session of the International Working Men's Association (IWMA, or First International) in spring 1866. Marx was not very much impressed with his new comrade. The problem was the young man's utopianism. Lafargue held to the Proudhonist doctrine that all 'nationalist' politicians whether romantic (Mazzini), reactionary (Bismarck) or revolutionary (Garibaldi) were fundamentally the same. Such a characteristically 'French' lumpen communism drew Marx's scorn. This is how he described one meeting of the International in a letter addressed to Frederick Engels in June 1866:

> The English laughed heartily when I began my SPEECH with the observation that our friend Lafargue, and others, who had abolished nationalities, had addressed us in '*French*', i.e. in a language which $^9/_{10}$ of the audience did not understand. I went on to suggest that by his denial of nationalities he seemed quite unconsciously to imply their absorption by the model French nation.[11]

Lafargue slowly adopted Marxist doctrines through conversations held during strolls on Hampstead Heath.[12] By the time of the 1867 congress of the International, Lafargue was in a position to second Marx's suggestion that the association should become 'a common centre of action for the working class'. The following year, Lafargue married Laura Marx, thus placing himself near the centre of the family. Both he and his wife corresponded with Marx and Engels, and both took on to defend the substance of Marx's socialism. Certainly when the French Socialist Workers' Party split in 1881, Lafargue played the role of defending Marxist orthodoxy. Paul Brousse's party, the 'Possibilists', came out in favour of municipal reform, theoretical diversity and national defence; while Paul Lafargue and Jules Guesde's 'Impossibilists' stood for revolution, Marxism and international solidarity.[13] The content of Lafargue's internationalism had developed, from a naïve belief in the 1860s that nations were a thing of the past, to his revolutionary claim of the 1880s that nationalism had to be fought.

During the period of the Second International, an orthodox socialist was someone who was loyal to a 'Marxism' developed in reading Marx, and through the interventions of Karl Marx himself, Friedrich Engels and then Karl Kautsky. Lafargue's socialism was criticised by his rivals in France precisely for such fidelity—it was far too 'German'. Leszek Kolakowski, the biographer of this generation, makes a similar criticism. He maintains that Lafargue was an economic determinist whose philosophy was closer to the late Feuerbach than Marx: 'In short, it cannot be said that Lafargue enlarged or improved upon Marxist doctrine in any way.'[14] Two responses come to mind. First, for the devotees of Marxist philosophy, it is true by definition that only philosophy matters. Such skills as the popularisation or development of existing theories do not count. Only originality is allowed. The best example of such creative thinking becomes that generation of Marxist philosophers, 'the children of Marx and Coca Cola', who have nicely reconciled Marxism with liberalism, every one of them announcing the same formula that 'grand narratives' (herds) are a thing of the past.[15] Second, the judgement of the philosophers is unfair to the man himself. Lafargue was a much more interesting and diverse thinker. Having come to scientific socialism late, and through admiration for both Proudhon and especially Auguste Blanqui (who Paul Lafargue met as a student activist), our author retained some of his old libertarian background.[16] The unusual combination of Marxism with pre-Marxist French socialism makes *The Right to Be Lazy* an interesting and unusual document to read.

As for the contradiction between the personal and the political, every socialist activist in history has encountered a tension between these two. This problem follows from the contradictions within the socialist project, which were raised at the very opening of this paper. The reason for becoming a socialist is that people want to see a different, equal society, without inhumanity and want. But stuck in a racist, sexist and capitalist world, it is impossible for anyone to escape to the future, and emancipate themselves thereby from the pressures to conform to the dictates of the present. Different writers and activists have resolved this tension keeping more or less of their dignity intact. Frederick Engels worked as a factory-manager, while Karl Marx owned shares, and Paul Lafargue had no better answers to these problems than anyone else. Moving towards the contents of his pamphlet, was Lafargue indolent in the way that *The Right to Be Lazy* demands? Certainly, Paul Lafargue was not a disciplined student, and his natural indolence helps to explain his failure to qualify as a doctor, at least as much as do the important distractions that he encountered on the revolutionary left.[17] After 1870, the death of his father rescued Paul Lafargue from the need to find paid employment. He settled down and became a diligent and prolific socialist journalist. Our hero was as disciplined as anyone, when the task was one he enjoyed.

Work: a strange madness

The Right to Be Lazy was a masterpiece of studied contempt. Lafargue relaxed his pen, and employed the satirist's skills of scorn and sarcasm, as he never had before. The structure of his first sentence owed something to the first line of the *Communist Manifesto*, 'A spectre is haunting Europe—the spectre of Communism'.[18] The difference is that in Paul Lafargue's account, the monstrous danger was something to be avoided, and not praised:

> A strange madness has taken possession of the working classes of those nations in which capitalist civilisation dominates. This madness brings in its wake the individual and collective sufferings which for two centuries have tortured an unhappy humanity. This madness is the love of work,

the destructive desire for labour, carried even to the extent of exhausting the vital forces of the individual and his offspring.[19]

For his negative model, Lafargue took the seventy-hour working week which was practised by so many people in late nineteenth-century France: 'Work, work, proletarians to augment social wealth and your individual misery. Work, work, so that becoming poorer you will have more reasons to work and be miserable. This is the inexorable law of capitalist production.'[20] In its place, Lafargue advocated leisure—not the wretched leisure industry of our day, but the emancipation of work through its re-integration into older patterns of short-work and frequent rest. 'The proletariat must constrain itself to work for no more than three hours a day and spend the rest of the day and night resting and banqueting.'[21]

One of the most distinctive themes of Lafargue's argument was his frequent use of classical and sometimes even older sources to praise an earlier world in which sustained leisure was seen as a higher good than permanent toil. The Bible was praised for the Sermon on the Mount ('Consider the lilies of the field, how they grow: they toil not neither do they spin'). Lafargue also cited the example given in Genesis—'the bearded Jehovah gave his followers the supreme example of ideal laziness: after six days' work, he rested for eternity'. There were also references to Antipatros, Cicero, Arcadian parrots, Venus, Herodotus ('even women were not allowed to spin or weave so as not to detract from their nobility'), Brutus the Elder, Tarquin, Plato, Xenophon ('work steals time'), Plutarch, Lycurgus and Daedalus. Lafargue praised to the skies the Greek ideal of civilised ease:

> The ancient Greeks had no more desire for work: free men practised only physical exercise and games of intelligence. This was the era when Aristotle, Phidias and Aristophanes moved and breathed among the people; when heroes at Marathon crushed the Asian hordes, who were also conquered by Alexander. The philosophers of Antiquity taught contempt for work—the degradation of the free man.[22]

You might conclude from this passage that Lafargue had been boning up on his classics, and we shall see that he had been doing just that.

A less attractive theme of *The Right to Be Lazy* was its author's confusion of matters of class and race. This point was never made explicit, nor was Lafargue arguing in defence of racial privilege, but like several other nineteenth-century writers, Paul Lafargue found it easiest when looking for a capitalist, to name a Jew. There are three references to Rothschild in this 15,000-word pamphlet, which is at least two more than any other banker or industrialist who came to Lafargue's mind. A similar disorder infects the passage, harmless in itself, in which he posed the question: 'for which races is work an organic necessity? The Auvergnians; the Scots (Auvergnians of the British Isles); Galicians (Spanish Auvergnians); Pomeranians (German Auvergnians); the Chinese (Asian Auvergnians).'[23] Was race really this important? The pamphlet makes no racist argument, nor was Paul Lafargue a recognisably racist writer—either by the standards of his day, or our own. Yet there is something crude here, which does not impress.[24]

Of more interest is Lafargue's attack on organised religion. As far as he was concerned, Christianity had justified slavery in antiquity and now it glorified alienated labour. Paul Lafargue had nothing bad to say against scripture, as we have seen. Yet our author had no good word to say for the work ethic of Protestantism, bemoaning the death of feudal work-practices in eighteenth-century Britain. Before the industrial revolution, by contrast, everything was fine: 'Morose England, immersed in Protestantism, was then known as "Merrie England".'[25] Nevertheless, Catholicism received even shorter shrift from Paul Lafargue's pen: 'Christian hypocrisy and capitalist utilitarianism didn't pervert the philosophers of the ancient Republics…The Bastiats, Dupanloups, Beaulieus and co with their Christian and capitalist morality, these thinkers and their philosophers recommend slavery.'[26] Such anti-clericalism was a common part of Paul Lafargue's socialism, certainly until the time of the Dreyfus affair, when it appears that secular intellectuals took over this target role.[27]

In the final few paragraphs of *The Right to Be Lazy*, Lafargue reminded his reader of the Greek philosopher Aristotle's desire that machinery would usher in a new era of human rest: 'if every tool could be used effortlessly, or move itself like the masterpieces of Daedalus or begin spontaneously their sacred work like Vulcan's tripods; if, for example, the weaver's shuttles did their own weaving, the head of the shop would not need any assistant, nor the master, slaves.' Lafargue endorsed this vision of technology, where human invention could be used to secure the ease people deserved. 'The genius of the great capitalist philosophers remains dominated by the prejudices of the salary, the worst slavery. They still don't understand that the machine is the redeemer of mankind, the God who will rescue humanity from the *sordidae artes* of wage slavery, the God who will give us leisure and liberty.'[28]

Origins of an idea

The success of *The Right to Be Lazy*, and the general absence of footnotes in the pamphlet, have encouraged historians to look for earlier manuscripts which acted as source-material for it. One influence could be the philosophy of Epicurus. He has been associated with the idea that a good life is a happy life—or as this philosophy has been understood in English, 'eat, drink and be merry, for tomorrow we die'. Indeed, Epicurus is no accidental figure to associate with the nineteenth-century left. Marx devoted his doctoral thesis to a comparison of the natural philosophies of Democritus and Epicurus, concluding heavily on the side of the latter.[29] A second potential source could be Lafargue's long-term influence, Pierre-Joseph Proudhon. The introduction to Proudhon's pamphlet *Sunday*, recommends leaving aside the 'discussion of work and wages, organisation and industry' in favour of the study of 'a law which would have at its basis a theory of rest'.[30] Another influence may have been Charles Fourier, whose work includes its own passionate critique of toil.[31] A fourth and most likely influence is Karl Marx. The message of Lafargue's pamphlet is close to the themes of Marx's earlier philosophical writings, including the *German Ideology* and his *1844 Manuscripts*.[32] Most of these remained unpublished until the twentieth century—but it is likely that some of the same themes recurred in those formative strolls along Hampstead Heath.

One source we know for certain, even though Lafargue declined to provide a reference. The very name of Lafargue's pamphlet was borrowed from Louis Moreau-Christophe's *The Right to Idleness and the Organisation of Slavery in the Greek and Roman Republics*.[33] Lafargue gently tweaked the phrase, to give his title a more provocative edge. No doubt Moreau-Christophe also provided the classical references. Our author came across the earlier book in the private library of Karl Marx, and was later sent Marx's original copy, following the older man's death in 1883.[34]

We cannot really know what Marx made of Moreau-Christophe's book, and still less can we know what opinions he passed on to his son-in-law. Yet Marx wrote several comments on his copy of this book. Many were aimed at Joseph Naudet, who wrote a critical afterword to Moreau-Christophe's original paper. Marx's marginal notes included a criticism of Naudet's belief that the law was a means to achieve justice: 'This proves that Naudet, although he cites the authors didn't understand the first word of Roman Law. Product, property—whose? That means law—whose? Force, armed theft or rapine.' Later Marx responded to Moreau-Christophe's defence of the duty to work, with a caustic aside worthy of Lafargue, observing that work is 'that which Christianity came to teach the world'.[35] Although these comments are interesting in themselves, sadly they do not constitute any 'missing link' to Lafargue's pamphlet. Paul Lafargue did not cite them in his text, and if he did ever read them, it can only have been after *The Right to Be Lazy* was already published.[36]

A pamphlet and a programme?

Over the past dozen years or so, several writers have sought a return to a pure set of left-wing values, a 'classical Marxism' unsullied by the defeat of the Russian revolution. The phrase 'classical Marxism' is taken from the Polish revolutionary, Isaac Deutscher, who was a supporter of Trotsky in exile and later became an inspiration to the New Left that grew up in the 1960s. Deutscher was very much an enthusiast for the Marxism of Lafargue's day, talking of the 'striking, and to a Marxist often humiliating contrast between what I call classical Marxism—that is, the body of thought developed by Marx, Engels, their contemporaries and after them by Kautsky, Plekhanov, Lenin, Trotsky, Rosa Luxemburg—and the vulgar Marxism, the pseudo-Marxism of the different varieties of European social-democrats, Stalinists, Kruschevites, and their like'.[37] Not everyone has been so friendly to the Marxists of the Second International. John Rees has condemned the lack of imaginative, dialectical thinking among several members of this generation, including especially Karl Kautsky.[38] It is hard to fit Paul Lafargue's into this debate. His significance is uneven, his presence contradictory. His other translated works lack the wit of *The Right to Be Lazy*. They are derivative and generally confirm the negative judgements given above.[39] Yet this pamphlet is Lafargue at his best. Its utopianism stands beyond the perspective of his contemporaries. The living essence of Marxism—the dialectical method—is there.

What about Lafargue's argument? In the one-hundred-plus years since the publication of Paul Lafargue's pamphlet, critical judgement has varied. *The Right to Be Lazy* has found unlikely enemies, and a few surprising champions as well. Among the unexpected critics can be counted the dissident Marxist Leszek Kolakowski, who was mentioned earlier. His claim is that Lafargue's socialism was a step backwards from classical Marxism. He suggests that the flaw of *The Right to Be Lazy* was that it described socialism purely in terms of consumption—'resting and banqueting'. Such 'hedonistic Marxism', according to Kolakowski, fails to explain what will happen when labour is no longer alienated. Even after the revolution, we will still need hospitals, schools, food and power supplies. So how will these be established, if nobody is going to do any work?[40] Lafargue gives two direct answers to this question in *The Right to Be Lazy*—the first is that the use of machinery should lead to greater leisure, the second is his acceptance of the need for a three-hour working day—yet both responses are insufficient as answers. On my reading of Paul Lafargue's pamphlet, a third and more compelling answer to Kolakowski's question is implied, although only lightly traced. I will return to this in a moment.

Among Paul Lafargue's surprising admirers can be counted the leaders of the last French government. In 1999 Lionel Jospin's socialists passed a new law introducing the 35-hour week. French workers already benefit from five weeks' paid holiday, two months' summer vacation, and a range of public holidays to make their confrères in Britain and America weep. Indeed Jospin has dropped his own hints suggesting the influence of Paul Lafargue on the new law.[41] Although Lafargue's general belief that shorter working hours could reduce unemployment may have influenced Lionel Jospin's coalition, the most compelling reason for introducing the law would perhaps have been to strengthen a Socialist Party challenged by three electoral blocs to its left— Trotskyists, Communists and Greens.

Between the crude ultra-left criticised by Kolakowski and the mild-mannered reformist beloved of Jospin, is there any space for the real Paul Lafargue to make himself known? One point is that Lafargue's claims are really not that exceptional. Even the physicist Albert Einstein, on those rare occasions when he gave substance to his socialist politics, spoke of the need to reduce the working week: 'In each branch of industry the number of working hours per week ought to be reduced by law so that unemployment is systematically abolished. At the same time minimum wages must be fixed in such a way that the purchasing power of the workers keeps pace with production.'[42] On this reading, the importance of Lafargue is that he reminds us of a basic truth which the left knew all along. The politics of Marx, the influence of Proudhon, the memory of the Paris Commune (during which Lafargue was a delegate-at-large in France), each of these influences can be traced in his book. The true originality of *The Right to Be Lazy* is that everyone else forgot to make these points in their propaganda, and it was left to Lafargue to fill the gap.

Kolakowski's challenge remains unanswered. If work is to be reduced, then what (in socialist theory) should take its place? It seems to me that the answer implied in Lafargue is the traditional Marxist answer. Certainly people will continue to produce after the revolution, but their labour will be different from 'work' as we understand it now. For one thing, there will be no class of employers, and no class of the employed. Therefore work will not be alien, in the sense that it will belong to the worker. Nobody will be expected to labour on tasks, which they have not chosen.[43] More fundamentally, the nature of employment will change. Similar ideas have been discussed by academics interested in educational theory. Thirty years ago Paulo Freire described education as a means to self-emancipation.[44] More recently, the most widely used concept has been 'play'. When educational writers use this word, they have in mind the unstructured learning of children in their first years. Individuals and groups develop rules without external compulsion. Education without rules, self-development and unconstrained learning, these are the ideals that writers have in mind.[45]

One author who has attempted to marry *The Right to Be Lazy* to play-theory is the libertarian socialist Bob Black. His web-tract, 'The Abolition of Work' follows closely the argument of Lafargue, 'Karl Marx's wayward son-in-law'. There are several unconvincing puns on 'ludic' game playing, but the content of Black's argument provides a serious answer to Kolakowski's challenge, mentioned above. Bob Black includes a useful definition of work (as 'forced labour') as well as a mapped-out alternative to it:

> What I really want to see is work turned into play. A first step is to discard the notions of a 'job' and an 'occupation'. Even activities that already have some ludic content lose most of it being reduced to jobs which certain people, and only those people, are forced to do to the exclusion of all else…Second, there are some things that people like to do from time to time, but not for too long, and certainly not all of the time…Third, other things being equal, some things are unsatisfying if done by yourself or in unpleasant surroundings or at the orders of an overlord, are enjoyable, at least for a while, if these circumstances are changed.[46]

The argument here is close to Lafargue's. To Black's account, we can add Lafargue's belief in mechanisation, and his notion of a remaining transitional three-hour day. The picture becomes clearer then and more consistent, the future more worked-out and more real.

Lafargue's notion of an easier future provides a compelling vision of the alternative society that most labour activists would actually like to bring about. Indeed his utopia would be compelling to much wider layers of people, even than that. Each year seems to bring new advances in labour-saving technology, but the working week never shortens—not for Spanish-speaking workers who are now challenging African-Americans to take on the roles of labourer, driver and cleaner for white urban America; not in Russia, where life expectancy has fallen over the past fifteen years; not in France where unemployment remains at ten per cent; and not in Britain where the gap between rich and poor has hardly narrowed in the hundred years since statistics were first collected. So much still needs to be done.

Notes

1. This book is republished in Karl Marx and Friedrich Engels, *Collected Works: Volume 25* (London, various dates), pp.5–312. Henceforth *MECW*.

2. The former appears in *MECW* 5, pp.19–539; the latter in *MECW* 22, pp.307–59.

3. *The State and Revolution* is republished in V. I. Lenin, *Collected Works: Volume 25* (London, 1964), pp.381–492.

4. See for example Oscar Wilde's, 'The Soul of Man under Socialism', reprinted in Oscar Wilde, *The Soul of Man and Prison Writings* (Oxford, 1990 edn), pp.1–37; and more recently, John Molyneux, *The Future Socialist Society* (London, 1997). Among the fantastic or science fiction Marxist utopias, I would mention I. M. Banks, *The Player of Games* (London: Orbit, 1988); K. MacLeod, *The Star Fraction* (London: Orbit, 1996); and William Morris, *News from Nowhere* (numerous editions).

5. To be pedantic, there are several Russian-sponsored classics, which have a title along these lines. One such is K. Marx, F. Engels, V. Lenin, *On Democracy— Bourgeois and Socialist* (Moscow, 1986). But the actual content of these collections is minimal. Short extracts are taken from the work of the founding fathers of Marxist theory, while long extracts are not used, for the reason (which I have already alluded to) that Marx, Engels and Lenin did not write sustained blue-prints for the future. Some of Trotsky's comments on the nature of socialism may however be found in his short book *Problems of Life* (London, 1924).

6. L. Derfler, *Paul Lafargue and the Founding of French Marxism, 1842–1882* (Cambridge, MA, 1991), p.181; also L. Derfler, *Paul Lafargue and the Flowering of French Socialism, 1882–1911* (Cambridge, MA, 1998).

7. Paul Lafargue, *The Right to Be Lazy*, ed. and trans. L. Bracken (Ardmore, PA, Fifth Season Press: 1999). Henceforth *RBL*. The French edition consulted for this article was Paul Lafargue, *Le droit à la paresse* (Paris, 1975). Henceforth *DLP*.

8. *RBL*, p.v.

9. The summary in this paragraph is loosely based on Sam Gordon's introduction to a projected but unpublished collection of Lafargue's pamphlets. This can be accessed at the *Revolutionary History* website, www.revolutionary-history.co.uk/.

10. Cited in *DLP*, p.103.

11. Marx to Engels, 20 June 1866, in *MECW* 42, pp.286–7.

12. P. Lafargue, 'Reminiscences of Marx', in E. Fromm, *Marx's Concept of Man* (New York, 1969), pp.221–41.

13. The issues are discussed in Derfler, *Lafargue*, pp.196–200.

14. Leszek Kolakowski, *Main Currents of Marxism: Its Rise, Growth and Dissolution, Volume II: The Golden Age* (Oxford, 1978), pp.141–50, here p.142.

15. Alex Callinicos, *Against Postmodernism* (Cambridge, 1989).

16. Lafargue's meeting with Blanqui is discussed in Derfler, *Lafargue and the Founding of French Marxism*, pp.28–31.

17. For correspondence between two concerned Victorian parents, see Marx to François Lafargue, 10 July 1889, in *MECW* 43, pp.314–15.

18. *MECW* 6, pp.483–96.
19. *DLP*, p.121.
20. *DLP*, p.129.
21. *DLP*, p.132. In French, the last phrase is the luxurious 'fainéanter et bombancer'.
22. *DLP*, pp.122–3.
23. *DLP*, p.123.
24. Lafargue is also taken to task in *RBL*, p.vii.
25. *DLP*, p.135.
26. *DLP*, p.152.
27. See for example, Lafargue's 'The Intellectuals', a 1900 speech translated by Charles Kerr, in *RBL*, pp.43–68.
28. *DLP*, p.152.
29. *MECW* 1, pp.25–108.
30. Derfler, *Lafargue and the Founding of French Marxism*, p.178. There is also a critical discussion of work in P.-J. Proudhon, *Qu'est-ce que la Propriété?* (Paris, 1849), pp.86–90.
31. T. Paquot, 'Le devoir de paresse', *Le Monde diplomatique*, April 1999, p.36.
32. The former appears in *MECW* 5, pp.19–539; the latter in *MECW* 3, pp.229–348.
33. L. Moreau-Christophe, 'Le droit à l'oisivité et de l'organisation du travail servile dans les Républiques grecque et romaine', paper presented to the Academy of Moral and Political Sciences, March-April 1849.
34. This entire episode is discussed in *DLP*, pp.96–9.
35. *Le Moniteur*, 4 June 1849.
36. *DLP*, p.99.
37. Isaac Deutscher, *Marxism, Wars and Revolutions* (London, 1984), p. 245.
38. John Rees, *The Algebra of Revolution: The Dialectic and the Classical Marxist Tradition* (London, 1998), pp.135–43.
39. P. Lafargue, *The Evolution of Property and Social and Philosophical Studies* (London, 1975).
40. Kolakowski, *Main Currents*, pp.147–8.
41. P. Webster, 'Idle Streak in the French Constitution', *Guardian*, 9 August 1999.
42. Although this sounds suspiciously like the Jospin incarnation of Lafargue, Einstein elsewhere committed himself to a more revolutionary socialism. The passage here is taken from 'Thoughts on the World Economic Crisis', in Albert Einstein *Ideas and Opinions* (New York, 1944 edn), pp.86–91. For the more radical Einstein, see 'Why Socialism?' in *Ideas and Opinions*, pp.151–8; and for a broader summary of Albert Einstein's socialism, David Renton, 'The Anti-fascist Politics of Albert Einstein', *Searchlight*, August 2000.
43. One important criticism of this argument is that it leaves no place for consumption. Revolutionary movements have tended to throw up directly-elected assemblies based often on people's situation in production (workers' councils), but sometimes also on their position as consumers (including women's

councils, city soviets, and the like). Probably the hardest challenge facing any socialist society worth of the name would be to establish a permanent consensus between these two groups.

44. P. Freire, *Pedagogy of the Oppressed* (London, 1996 edn).
45. L. Holzman, 'Stop Working and Get to Play', *Lib Ed* 23–4 (1994), pp.8–12.
46. This article can be accessed at www.carney.com.erik/. Its author states that '*The Abolition of Work* is anticopyright and may be freely reproduced even without mentioning the source.'

Reviews

Books to be remembered (7)

T. E. B. Howarth, *Cambridge Between Two Wars,* London, 1978

This is a well-informed volume which offers material on many different aspects of university life. The text is divided between the 1920s and 1930s and each part has three main sections: 'Men, women and manners'; 'The advancement of learning'; and 'Politics'. The author had an active war service, being awarded the Military Cross and later becoming Personal Liaison Officer to Montgomery in North Western Europe. After the war he went into teaching and became High Master of St Paul's School, London (it was his old school) and then, in 1973, he was appointed Senior Tutor at Magdalene College, Cambridge. He died in 1988, when his *Times* obituary notice included the interesting, if somewhat unusual, observation: 'Both as a don and as a schoolmaster, he was either loved or loathed.'

Whatever his personal characteristics, he wrote as a liberal-minded Conservative and his book is well-organised with considerable detail. There are some interesting accounts of different social attitudes: the matter of women students, for example. Girton and Newnham were well-established, having in 1881 been admitted into the Tripos examinations, although not allowed to use the titles of the degrees they had passed. Attempts to change this rule had failed before 1914 and in the years immediately before 1918 the matter became of significant debate, with many senior members of the university now in favour of change. But there were not enough of them. In the spring of 1919 a committee was formed to decide upon the position of women. As it turned out, there were six Conservatives and six Liberals in its composition. The Liberal report recommended that women should be admitted to full membership but excluded from men's colleges. The Conservative report suggested the establishment of a women's university, centred at first upon Girton and Newnham. Senate, in December, rejected the Liberal report by a vote of 904 to 712. Oxford, it should be noted, had by this time admitted women to full membership, a decision approved by Convocation without a vote. The women in Cambridge slowly marched on, the first women professor being installed on the eve of the Second World War.

There are some interesting personal stories. J. B. S. Haldane's divorce is one. Haldane was a brilliant biochemist with some personal habits that many found difficult to accept. Trinity gave him a bed and dining rights but never made him a Fellow. In 1924 he fell in love with Charlotte Burghes, whose husband refused to give her grounds for divorce. So, within the existing divorce laws, he and Charlotte found it necessary to commit adultery in an overt manner. Haldane made no secret of what he intended, and in due course his case was considered by the *Sex Viri*, the group within the university responsible for morals and social behaviour. His conduct was judged one of gross immorality and it was recommended that he be deprived of his Readership. Haldane appealed and his case was upheld.

The 1930s in Cambridge politics were no different from other academic institutions. Cambridge had been moving only slowly from its pre-war attitudes in the years which followed the mass killings of the First World War. It is a matter of some surprise that the immediate years after 1918 showed no serious reaction in political terms against the horrors that affected such large numbers of British people. There was C. E. Montague's *Disenchantment* which was published in 1924, but not until the closing years of the decade did there appear a growing body of anti-war literature that was to have a profound effect upon public opinion. The collective influence of writings like R. C. Sheriff's *Journey's End* or Remarque's *All Quiet on the Western Front*—the list could be much extended—and the poetry of Siegfried Sassoon, Wilfred Owen and others, was remarkable upon most areas of public life.

It was in 1934 that the Peace Pledge Union was established, and in the same period the League of Nations Union organised a national ballot relating to collective security, disarmament and sanctions against aggressors. Eleven million voted, with the overwhelming majority in favour of large-scale disarmament and sanctions against those involved in aggression. The influence of these new attitudes is given some space by Howarth but he has missed this large outpouring of anti-war writing. Instead, he tends to concentrate, in his analysis of the changes of opinion, especially from within the student population, upon the new and growing impact of the Soviet Union and the concomitant increase of interest in Marxist ideas. He is clear about certain of the absurdities of left opinion in these years, but he offers too little emphasis upon the anti-war sentiment or the impact of fascism with the coming of Hitler. This decade of the 1930s is admittedly complicated for the historian, and Howarth is helpful only in part. Very correctly, he gives proper emphasis to the Spanish Civil War, and in particular to the deaths of John Cornford, David Haden Guest and Julian Bell in the struggle against Franco.

There is much in this volume for the scientist, and the social scientist. These were years when Cambridge included some famous names in most of the general areas of research. In pure and applied science there were Rutherford, Kapitza, Haldane, Bernal, Blackett, Needham, J. D. Cockcroft, Eddington, Gowland Hopkins, and in the social sciences Maynard Keynes, Wittgenstein and some interesting historians. The author's chapters on the advancement of learning are consistently interesting.

There is no other volume that can be directly compared with this (or perhaps I have missed another book to be remembered). Similar analyses of other periods of institutions would without question be of great importance for the fuller intellectual history of twentieth-century Britain.

John Saville

John Saville, *Memoirs From The Left* (London, Merlin Press, 2003), 197pp., ISBN 0-8503-6520-1, £14.95 pbk.

John Saville is an eminent member of a brilliant group of Marxist historians who have contributed so much to the renaissance of social and labour history. A charismatic and dynamic figure, Saville has not only written much very good history but has also been a notable academic entrepreneur. He has edited three volumes of *Essays in Labour History* with Asa Briggs, ten volumes of the *Dictionary of Labour Biography* with Joyce Bellamy (1966–99) as well as *The Reasoner* and *The New Reasoner* with E. P. Thompson and *The Socialist Register* with Ralph Miliband.

From his undergraduate days at the LSE until 1956 Saville was a dedicated member of the Communist Party of Great Britain. He spent much of his second year at the LSE as organiser of the communist group there and he appears to have been assiduous in making contact with the local communist officials when he was moved around in the army. Before the Second World War he eagerly took instruction from the writings of Rajani Palme Dutt and, present at RAF unrest in 1945, he apparently was 'clear [that] only the Party group could offer the kind of sensible, well thought out political leadership that the situation demanded' (p.69). His party activities, not least in India during the Second World War, were a major focus in his life.

Hence, for John Saville, as for so many others, the break with the Communist Party of Great Britain in 1956 was the major personal political upheaval of his life. He devotes one of his six chapters to it. He wanted the British party to acknowledge its mistakes during the Stalin era and he argued that members needed an open discussion, with 'serious theoretical analysis of why, in a socialist society, these things should have happened' (pp.105–6). Failing to secure a CPGB led open debate, John Saville and E. P. Thompson facilitated intellectual debate by producing the Reasoner, which had under its heading a quotation from Marx, 'To leave error unrefuted is to encourage intellectual immorality'. Their continuing publication of the Reasoner led to their resignation from the CPGB and to the publishing of the New Reasoner, which was merged with universities and *Left Review* to form *New Left Review* in 1960.

John Saville has remained a Marxist but without a party. He was hostile to Trotskyism and unwilling to join the Labour Party. His memoirs make clear his problems in desiring both a disciplined vanguard party yet a democratic one. Looking back in these memoirs, reaffirming that he remains a Marxist, he observed:

But the most difficult problem, which has greatly affected the history of all socialisms in the twentieth century, is the question of organisation, and the extent to which intellectual leadership can move down to the rank and file of the membership, and remain acceptable. I remain unclear on a number of issues relevant to this central question...(p.165).

His memoirs provide a thoughtful account of one who believed, resigned from the party, yet still has much of his communist faith intact. He is vigorous in his views on the CPGB, taking particular exception to Raphael Samuel's 'The Lost World of Communism' series of articles which he dubs 'a rambling and often inchoate political sociology' (pp.8-9). His memoirs are a fascinating and substantial addition to communist party autobiography, ranging from the LSE to the British army in India to the crisis of faith of 1956.

Yet there is far more to his memoirs than reminisces and reflections on communism. His time in the army was one of the most memorable, and perhaps most enjoyable, of his life. Another vanguardism? He was pro-active and enjoyed leadership. The importance of these years to him comes over in these memoirs as strongly as it did when he gave an autobiographical talk to a conference held in Manchester on Labouring Lives in 2001.

Another major theme is his role in promoting labour and social history. He was a member of the Communist Party's Historians' Group. He rightly observes, 'No one...in 1939 would have expected the historians to be the liveliest intellectual group within the Communist Party in the immediate post-war decade' (p.86). It was. John Saville had initially been closest to James Jefferys. He later saw more of E.P and Dorothy Thompson. He tells with pleasure how he recommended an editor of a book series to go to E.P. Thompson, with the publication of *The Making of the English Working Class* being the outcome. He was a founder member and a leading figure in both the Society for the Study of Labour History and the Oral History Society. Perhaps John Saville's finest hours as a historian came with retirement, with such books as *The British State and the Chartist Movement* (1987) and *The Politics of Continuity. British Foreign Policy and the Labour Government 1945–1946* (1993).

John Saville's memoirs also recount the curious episode of an MI5 agent who spied on him from 1959, as an eminent figure of the 'New Left'. The man went on to CND and the Institute of Workers' Control. A notable feature of this sad story is that the man was launched from an adult training college with trade union connections. This was a feature of the 1960s; adult education being a way to get men and women into the student and trade union movements. I think that army intelligence used Birkbeck College in 1968 as a way to infiltrate the student left while it is quite possible that the CIA used the student European Movement for the same purposes. Whether I am right or wrong will be shown long after I am dead, unless the Blair government actually delivers on its promised Freedom of Information Act.

Although there is some repetition in these memoirs, generally they are lean and stylish. John Saville has always been intellectually curious and his breadth of interest comes through. There is some self-awareness. He even regrets not getting to know Roy Hattersley when he was a student, observing 'I would guess it was my political sectarianism that kept me from getting closer to him' (p.153). He pays tribute to Joyce Bellamy, who was something of a saint to work so long in an academic partnership with him; yet it is a pity he needs to provide a blunt assessment of what he feels to have been her theoretical shortcomings.

Overall, this is a memorable autobiography, providing a recognisable portrait of its subject. John Saville has always been energetic and determined. Even in his eighties he has bustled along, working vigorously at several enterprises at once, and leaving much younger people behind in his wake, much impressed by his drive, ability and general benevolent disposition.

Chris Wrigley
former chairperson of the Society for the Study of Labour History and
Professor of History at the University of Nottingham

Paul Preston, *Doves of War: Four Women of Spain* (London, HarperCollins, 2002), x+469pp., ISBN 0-00-255633-2, £16.99 hbk.

Paul Preston makes clear from the outset that *Doves of War* has no 'theoretical pretensions. Its objective is quite simple—to tell the unknown stories of four remarkable women whose lives were starkly altered by their experiences in the Spanish Civil War' (p.7). Much then rests on the intrinsic interest of the lives described in these four biographical essays—a format that Preston has already successfully employed in his *Comrades!* (1999). The first story, that of Priscilla (Pip) Scott Ellis, whose civil war diary was published in 1995, is also the slightest. Scott Ellis came from a wealthy English family that enjoyed close links with the Spanish royal family. These connections helped her to volunteer as a nurse on Franco's side, a decision that was also influenced by her unrequited love for Prince Ataúlfo de Orléans who was serving with the German Condor Legion. There is no doubting Pip's courage as a front-line nurse, nor the sadness of her private life when, following the civil war, she married the exploitative Josè Luis de Villalonga. However, as hardly any other British women volunteered to serve on Franco's side, her story is inevitably a somewhat isolated one. It is perhaps best seen as representative of the divided loyalties that many on the right in Britain must have felt as war with Nazi Germany (and possibly also with Franco's Spain) loomed in the late 1930s.

The essay on Nan Green carries a far greater resonance given the current vogue for biographical studies of the communist movement. Green had joined the British Communist Party with her musician husband George in the early 1930s. In 1937 first George and then Nan went to Spain to join the Republican side (Wogan Philipps having paid for their two young children to be educated at Summerhill School). Although Nan's story is already reasonably well known, Preston tells it extremely well, enlivening his narrative with some remarkable letters from the family archive. He argues that Nan's brief affair with a British volunteer while working in a hospital in Spain left her with lifelong feelings of guilt, especially as George was to die soon afterwards in the battle of the Ebro (just before the International Brigades were withdrawn from the front line). He deals relatively briefly with the remainder of her life, including her work in China in the 1950s, her failed marriage to Ted Brake, and her prominent role in the International Brigade Association (IBA). Relying on Green's unpublished memoirs, written towards the end of her life, Preston argues that following George's death Nan became a 'more serious and single-minded Party militant' (p.178) who suppressed her growing doubts about communism. The evidence from archival sources does not, however, always fit neatly with this interpretation. For instance, in 1942 her appointment as secretary of the IBA was initially blocked due to lingering doubts amongst some Communist Party leaders about her political reliability, doubts which had first surfaced in Spain. Archival sources also lead one to question Preston's comment that Green found the USSR's split with Yugoslavia 'distressing' (p.194). In fact, within the IBA she was an opponent of those who felt that solidarity with fellow Yugoslav International Brigaders should transcend the rift within international communism.

The final essays deal with two Spanish women who struggled to establish a leadership role during the Civil War. The chapter on the Socialist Party (PSOE) politician Margarita Nelken is the most rounded in the book, not least because she is the best-known of these four women, and a far greater range of sources is available on her life. Nelken was a highly intelligent and cultured woman who had already made a reputation as a writer, art critic and feminist before winning a 1931 by-election to become a PSOE deputy. She was a passionate defender of the southern farm labourers during the Second Republic, and increasingly drifted towards revolutionary politics. Her fierce rhetoric earned her the hatred of the right and a period in exile. At the start of the Civil War Nelken rallied the Republican militias against the Nationalist forces marching on Madrid, and bravely remained in the capital after the government had fled. However, as Preston makes clear, her political career was ruined by her ill-judged decision to join the Communist Party at a time when there was no clear role for her to play within it. With the defeat of the Republic she was forced to flee to France, and eventually settled in Mexico where she worked to look after her extended family. The latter part of Nelken's life was scarred by the tragic death of her beloved son in 1944 (fighting in the Red Army) and of her daughter ten years later, while her expulsion from the Communist Party in 1942 exposed her to bitter invective from former allies. Preston tells the harrowing story of her grief-stricken final years with great compassion.

Preston's fourth subject is Mercedes Sanz-Bachiller, the widow of the fascist leader Onésimo Redondo who was killed in action soon after the start of the conflict. Undaunted, Sanz-Bachiller embarked on creating a voluntary social welfare organisation inspired by the Nazi 'Winter Help'. She rose to be one of the best-known leaders of Nationalist Spain, enjoying good relations with Franco. However, she fell foul of the internal politics of the Falangist movement, and especially of Pilar Primo de Rivera, who saw her as a rival. Preston records her rise, fall and eventual rehabilitation under the Franco regime with great attention to detail and a commendable objectivity. Her story reinforces the simple but powerful message of *Doves of*

War—that the Spanish Civil War imposed heavy emotional costs on women, victors and vanquished alike. The death of sons and husbands, the disruption of normal family life, and the guilt associated with survival are all to be found in this book. Equally, Preston shows how able women struggled to find a role within a male-dominated public sphere. Both Sanz-Bachiller and Nelken, for instance, suffered from the perception that there was only room for one powerful woman in their respective political movements. This is not a particularly ambitious book, but Preston's mastery of this style of biographical writing, as well as his profound knowledge of the Civil War and its aftermath, mean that it deserves a wide readership.

Tom Buchanan
Lecturer in Modern History and Politics, OUDCE, Oxford

Archie Potts, *Zilliacus: A Life for Peace and Socialism* (London, Merlin Press, 2002), ISBN 0 85036 509 0, £14.95 pbk.

This is the first full-scale biography of Konni Zilliacus—internationalist, League of Nations official, prolific journalist, tireless pamphleteer for peace and, latterly, Labour MP and leading critic of Cold War British foreign policy.

Given his background Zilliacus could hardly have been anything but an internationalist. He was born in 1894 in Japan of Swedo-Finnish descent. His father was an energetic figure in the anti-Czarist agitation and the struggle for Finnish independence. Educated in Sweden, Finland, the USA, England, and then at Yale University, Zilliacus was radicalised by his experience at the British Consulate at Vladivostock during the allied intervention. He returned from this posting a committed internationalist, joined the Labour Party and secured employment in Geneva with the League of Nations, working in the Information Section of the League Secretariat. From here, he remained in touch with key figures in the Labour Party, and played a behind-the-scenes role in getting the Party to adopt a pro-League of Nations foreign policy.

Zilliacus was no pacifist, and advocated a firm international response (which never materialised) to Japan's advance into Manchuria, believing that a concerted international response would deter Japanese adventurism. The failure to enforce the League Covenant in this case, he felt, was a betrayal of all that it stood for. Increasing international tensions in the second half of the 1930s also saw the beginnings of Zilliacus's differences over foreign policy with the Labour elite. Whereas Bevin and Dalton came to advocate rearmament in the face of growing German military strength, Zilliacus felt it unnecessary in view of the 'pooled' military strength of the League. Moreover, the seeming indifference of Dalton et al to the Republican cause in the Spanish Civil War infuriated Zilliacus. He later reflected that: 'Labour's behaviour over Spain...denoted not only a political but a moral and intellectual failure on the part of its leaders'. By the eve of the Second World War, largely as a result of his consistent advocacy of resolving international disputes through an activist League, Zilliacus found himself more aligned with the Left-wing critics of Labour policy rather than, as previously, being on the inside and exerting influence over it.

In 1938 he resigned from the League and returned to England, producing an avalanche of journalism on the international situation, speaking at countless public meetings, and becoming the Labour candidate for the Gateshead constituency. After working in the Ministry of Information throughout the War, in 1945 at 50 years of age, Zilliacus was elected to Parliament. From here Zilliacus would have been bitterly disappointed with the direction of Bevin's foreign policy were it not for the fact that he expected nothing more of Bevin. Nevertheless, his criticism further isolated him from the figures—including Attlee—who he had been close to in the pre-War period. He wasn't helped by the fact that he was a natural loner, isolated in Parliament and generally lumped together with figures like John Platts-Mills and Leslie Solley. What some regarded as his Sovietphilia during the period of the emerging Cold War added to his isolation. At times Zilliacus appeared naïve with regard to the Soviet Union (for example, over the creation of the Cominform and the autonomy that local communist parties would supposedly enjoy), and his failure to speak out over the 1948 coup in Czechoslovakia further isolated him from a largely horrified Labour Left. While his friendship with Tito suggested he was no mere apologist for the Soviet Union, he famously appeared as a witness in a court case in Paris brought by Soviet defector Victor Kravchenko, after the French Communist weekly, *Les Lettres Françaises*, claimed that such was the anti-Soviet bias in his autobiography, *I Chose Freedom*, that it must have been ghost-written by American Intelligence, to explain away Stalinist excesses. Here, Zilliacus told the court that the collectivisation of agriculture was necessary on economic grounds, that the purges of the 1930s had rooted out a potential fifth column, and that the Nazi-Soviet Pact had been used by Stalin to strengthen Soviet defences. His preference for taking his holidays east of Ipswich did little to counter the impression that his sympathies were more pro-communist than pro-Labour, and in 1949 he was expelled from the Party.

Readmitted to the Party in 1952, Zilliacus was elected MP for Gorton in 1955, and served the constituency until his death in 1967. During this period he became closely associated with CND and the campaign against nuclear weapons. Although an active journalist, tireless and popular speaker, and early revisionist historian of the Cold War (*I Choose Peace*), in Parliament Zilliacus was more isolated than ever. Nevertheless, he remained a perceptive critic of Anglo-American foreign policy, and despite ill-health was a constant thorn in the side of the Wilson government over Vietnam.

Konni Zilliacus displayed a complete absence of personal political calculation or ambition which sometimes verged on naivety, as did certain of his personal political judgements. However, this should not obscure the fact that Zilliacus remained primarily an internationalist, and that his interventions in print, in parliamentary debates, and at Labour conferences were ultimately based on support for the UN Charter, and on the world community acting in concert to deal with threats to peace, as opposed to attempting to isolate the socialist experiment in the Soviet Union. It was this hostility towards it, Zilliacus believed, that accounted for many of its more unpleasant features. It therefore followed that a relaxation of tension would bring positive results.

Archie Potts has provided a biography that highlights the many virtues of Konni Zilliacus, but also his flaws. Although it only deals with the later parliamentary period comparatively briefly, it is the fullest biography of Zilliacus we are likely to get, or indeed require. It should help ensure that his contribution to the debate about Labour foreign policy in the twentieth century gets the full credit it deserves.

Mark Phythian
University of Wolverhampton

K.D.M. Snell and Paul Ell, *Rival Jerusalems: The Geography of Victorian Religion* (Cambridge, Cambridge University Press, 2000), 516pp., ISBN 0 521 77155 2, £60.00

British religious history has, until recently, hardly been the focus of most socialist historians. Protestant non-conformity for example seemed to be of interest to the left only to the extent that it prevented a secular proletarian revolution or contributed to the establishment of the British trade union movement. Yet the stubborn persistence of popular religious belief into the twentieth century has seemed curiously at odds with confident predictions of universal secularisation. Over the past twenty years, the influence of the *Annales* school, Foucault, feminism and the 'new cultural history' has led to a reassessment of the role of religion in modern British history. As Carolyn Ford has observed, there is now a new interest in finding out more about 'the persistence of popular religious enthusiasm…the relationship between popular religion and politics…and the larger social and cultural meanings of spiritual belief.'

This sea change in religious historiography is acknowledged in K. D. M. Snell and Paul Ell's new work, *Rival Jerusalems*, when in their opening, they pay tribute to the insights of George Eliot's *Silas Marner*. Eliot, they tell us, unlike a number of historians who later wrote on the subject, was not only sensitive to the cultural significance of religion but also discerned the significance of regional differences in nineteenth-century religious observance.

Rival Jerusalems is a methodologically ambitious book which, despite its opening homage to imaginative literature, is much more interested in establishing technologically transparent methods of recovering useable evidence from disparate types of historical sources. What the authors aim to do is to establish both the insights of the novelist and the impressionistic assertions of previous religious historians, in a solid, statistically based, analysis of the spatial distribution of religious affiliation. Purporting to offer 'the fullest quantitative and cartographic research ever conducted into the contexts of British religion' from the late seventeenth to the mid-nineteenth centuries, the authors challenge the easy generalisations about Britain's national religious character, by focusing precisely on its regional differences. Using the 1676 Compton Census and the 1851 Religious Census as their starting point for comparison, they employ sophisticated computer analysis, to delve into the records of over 2400 parishes and all 624 registration districts in England and Wales in order to chart the correlations between socio-economic and demographic factors and religious observance.

Whilst many of its findings only confirm what we vaguely knew already, (e.g. that non-conformity was stronger in the North and West than in the South and East), some of its conclusions still have the power to excite surprise. Most notably, the religious geography of Wales in the period under study was found to have a greater coherence and to have been more distinct from that of England's (even accounting the considerable regional variations within England) than had previously been realised. For example, fewer than 5 per cent of Merthyr Tydfil's 'proportion share' (a measure of religious allegiance based on the number of seats, attendances and numbers of places of worship) in 1851 was Anglican. By the same (complicated, but we are assured, reliable) statistical measure, Welsh Anglicans averaged out at under 30 per cent of the total as compared to the English national average of 53 per cent. This probably explains much about Welsh identity and political behaviour and opens up some intriguing new research areas. And if few will be astonished that secularisation tended to flourish in large urban areas, they may be interested to learn that it also tends to occur in border regions where local identities are less coherent and more open to alternative constructions. 'Cultural diversity,' we are told, 'whether very urban, or in the form of the ambivalent loyalties and poor provision of the very rural Welsh and Scottish borderlands, proved uncongenial to religious attendance' and to religious affiliation more generally. Yet, any simple causal link between urbanity and secularisation is also challenged since even the Anglican Church was found to flourish in certain urban areas if other factors were 'right'.

The thoroughness and scope of this investigation will make it the authoritative touchstone for researchers in the field. Unfortunately for less specialist readers, its precision is often achieved at the expense of clarity and flow. The more methodologically innovative the chapters, the denser the prose. Nevertheless, undergraduates will still profit from reading the admirably clear (if not terribly exciting) accounts of the nature, status and spatial dispositions of Old and New Dissent. The differences between, for example English Presbyterianism and Independency, are lucidly put forward. The chapter on Roman Catholicism and Irish immigration is full of fascinating data about the pre- and post-famine Catholic communities. Again, many in the field will not learn much that is new in terms of content, but the new methods employed add precision and authority to old impressions.

Such precision too, can add weight to national generalisations whilst at the same time making the case for the importance of regional variations. The authors subject the Tillyard thesis, which argued that Methodism was strongest in England where Old Dissent was weak, to critical scrutiny. Tillyard's overall conclusions are vindicated but the authors' approach also substantiates those regional anomalies, whose existence had previously been asserted on the basis of literary or anecdotal evidence alone.

This is a beautifully produced and carefully conceived book. The authors state at the outset what they can and cannot cover and readers are promised a fuller discussion of secularisation in a forthcoming study by their colleague Alasdair Crockett. But the authors are in part limited by the conceptual limitations of the sources they exploit. This is a book about England and Wales and not Scotland, in large part because Scotland did not have registration units comparable to those used for England and Wales in the 1851 census. This is a book too, specifically about *Christian* observance, the Jews are left out, partly because of confusions about which groups were classed as Jewish in the 1851 census, and partly (and less convincingly) because 'they [the Jews] are admirably treated by others.' Whilst at one level, this makes methodological sense, it seems a shame the authors could not draw upon this 'admirable' scholarship to enrich their own discussions about the nature of the relationship between socio-economic factors, political behaviour and cultural identity in England and Wales. Even less understandable is their omission of any discussion of sexual difference, let alone gender, in religious observance. Even in the introduction, this dimension seems completely ignored, despite the pioneering work of Clive Field, Deborah Valenze, Phyllis Mack, Gail Malmgreen et al, and despite the authors' own declaration that 'the stress throughout is on the contextual understanding of religion'. One wonders what the author of *Adam Bede* and *Daniel Deronda* would have thought about such omissions in this otherwise admirable book.

Madge Dresser
University of the West of England

John McIlroy, Kevin Morgan, Alan Campbell (eds), *Party People, Communist Lives: Explorations in Biography* (Lawrence & Wishart, London, 2001), 256pp., ISBN 0 85315 936 X, £19.99 pbk.

As Kevin Morgan makes clear in his excellent contribution to *Party People, Communist Lives*, the history of the Communist Party of Great Britain (and international communism generally) has been ill served in terms of biography. With regard to Britain, only Harry Pollitt, Rajani Palme Dutt and Shapurji Saklatvala have received extensive biographical attention, while the lives of international communist activists beyond the Soviet Union have only just begun to command serious study. The reasons for this are multiple. Most obviously, access to much of the necessary research material has been beyond reach until relatively recently. Yet, communist biography has also been hindered by the very nature of its subject. The avowed uniformity (or monolithicity) of the communist movement, coupled with the subsequent subservience of the individual to 'the party', has tended to render communist biography (and autobiography) difficult and, for some, undesirable. For the Cold Warriors of both the right and the left, the need to *judge* communism has necessarily led to an approach that squeezes the individual into an already fixed model of totalitarian oppressiveness. According to Ralph Darlington, at least, 'personal idiosyncrasies' are irrelevant to our understanding of a person's political development. Simultaneously, communist writers have themselves buried their own or others' lives beneath the requirements of party discipline and the collective class struggle. Previous autobiographies and hagiographies of party members have sought to present a template for others to follow, not an objective study inclusive of a person's personal foibles.

For Morgan, however, the biographical approach facilitates a fresh, instructive and rewarding perspective on communism. It raises questions of human agency to set against the institutional bias of most historical studies, revealing the complexities of a communist life that moves away from (or at least tests) the stereotypical Stalinist automaton generally presented. The product, as Morgan states, is often a far more 'complex, nuanced and unsettling account'. Here, the individual is located in a 'series of temporal, spatial, social and institutional contexts whose precise inter-relationships distinguish that individual and help explain the dramas and dilemmas of that particular life'. To this effect, the impressive Communist Biographical Project orchestrated by the editors of *Party People* has paved the way for a history of communism that balances, explores and assesses the interplay between the personal, political, social and cultural. Moreover, it has allowed attention to be focused on those beyond the ranks of the party hierarchy to thereby broaden our understanding of the communist experience. The 'big issues' remain—such as a communist's relationship to crimes of Stalinism and the extent of Moscow's 'control' over history—but they are placed within a context irreducible to neat monocausal explanation.

Accordingly, the biographical studies collected in *Party Lives* reveal the diverse characters and experiences of just a few of the many who passed through the CPGB's ranks in the period preceding the Second World War. We are presented with a series of 'communisms', as different people interpreted their commitment to the party, the Communist International, the USSR and the working class in a variety of different ways. The book moves from genteel middle class drawing rooms and bohemian London to the pit villages of Scotland and Wales, taking in both party members steeped in the traditions of the broader British labour movement and those drawn to the party by the possibilities occasioned by the Russian revolution. Similarly, we see a range of journeys to and sometimes from communism. As a result, multiple narratives emerge, revealing an often complex relationship between party and comrade. The 69-year-old Dora Montefiore's conversion to communism came from a long political life dedicated to the struggle against social inequality, bringing with her perspectives and traditions that both informed and potentially challenged the conceptions of the CPGB. Like Rose Smith, too, Montefiore had to carve a role for herself in the face of gender relations informed as much by tradition as by the progressive rhetoric of official party policy. The four mining leaders included—Arthur Horner, Willie Allan, David Proudfoot and Abe Moffat—each had to reconcile their communist objectives with the practical realities of the coalfield, while Jack Gaster found himself in a party that had previously dismissed him as an 'insufferable petty bourgeois' member of the ILP. If there is one complaint about the collection, however, it is that there is a slight overemphasis on middle class members that belies the overwhelmingly proletarian basis of the party. Of the ten principal comrades discussed, four (Dora Montefiore, Arthur Reade, Randall Swindler, Jack Gaster) came from middle- to upper middle-class backgrounds. Even so, the relationship between these bourgeois converts to communism and the proudly proletarian CPGB is in itself a fascinating sub-theme running through *Party Lives*.

Of course, parallels can be drawn. For all of the biographical subjects, the Soviet Union represented a beacon of hope and inspiration at some time in their lives, and they all came to accept (even if only temporarily) the primacy of Bolshevism within the socialist tradition. In such a way, each of the featured comrades negotiated their lives as a communist via the theoretical strictures drafted and enforced by Moscow and the Communist International. Indeed, as Barry McLoughlin's essay on British comrades' encounters with the Soviet bureaucracy makes clear, this could often lead to terrifying and life-changing situations. The wider connotations of this, and the extent to which it shaped British history, remains a moot point. What these biographies suggest is that the lives of British communists cannot, and should not, be wholly divorced from their indigenous circumstance. If the Soviet element represented an important part of a communist's life, it did not prevent tensions and simultaneously competing or contradictory factors from shaping an individual's personal and political history.

Overall, *Party Lives* is an insightful and fascinating collection. Hopefully, it will be the first of many publications emerging from the Biographical Project, and an inspiration for researchers looking to formulate new approaches to communism both in Britain and abroad.

Matthew Worley
University of Reading

Julie V. Gottlieb, *Feminine Fascism: Women in Britain's Fascist Movement, 1923–1945* (London, I.B. Tauris, 2000), ISBN 1 86064 544 5, £39.50 hbk.

Despite historians' interest in British fascism, the role of women within the movement has been relatively neglected. Male fascists have been accorded more attention both in the 1930s and by posterity because of the extreme masculinity of the leader of the British Union of Fascists (BUF), Sir Oswald Mosley, and because of BUF's reputation as 'a para-military organization motivated by the masculine and macho ethos' (p.1). Building on the work of a few pioneers such as Martin Durham, Julie Gottlieb has produced a balanced, nuanced and thoroughly researched study of feminine fascism that shows such neglect to have been undeserved. Her book helps to illuminate the shortcomings of British party politics from the female point of view. It also establishes the distinctiveness of the British fascist movement, and the impossibility of combining feminism and fascism. Along the way, the many paradoxes inherent in feminine fascism are skilfully highlighted.

Thus in a movement associated with the rejection of pacifism, women activists were determinedly involved in a peace campaign to avert British conflict with Germany. Women were needed and rewarded in a new political organisation; but whilst there was some gender co-operation, they did not secure the top jobs—the key policy making roles. The programme of British fascism attracted young women, yet it also drew women with prior movement experience and assumptions. Despite fascism's apparent appeal for youth, many female supporters were entirely hostile to the 'new woman' and modernism, as they were commonly represented. Whereas fascists emphasised their cross-class orientation, middle and upper-class women were actually to the fore. And if some fascist women denounced feminism, and the anti-suffrage tradition was integrated within the BUF, ex-suffragettes were among its members and the union was at pains to repudiate the accusation of anti-feminism. As one would expect, these paradoxes aggravated the dissent and regrouping which were a feature of the British fascist campaign.

Although the author makes clear her own disapproval of the fascist mentality and agenda, she sets her work firmly in context, and neither judges feminine fascists according to the tenets of modern feminism nor suggests that they were driven primarily by gender considerations. Consequently, her discussion of women fascists' ideas on gender is particularly persuasive. They—like interwar feminists—grappled with the tension between women's distinctiveness and their desire for equality, balancing respect for women's right to employment outside the home with admiration for female selflessness, especially displayed in the maternal commitments which they and the state greatly valued. But, equally, fascist women were little consulted about the BUF's racialist pronatalism; were not necessarily expected to benefit from the party's equal pay proposal (which might exclude them from employment); and were urged to accept both that they were already emancipated, and that they could never obtain equality with men in spheres to which they were unsuited. An interesting case is made for a link between fascism and the suffragette movement, both of them militant, anti-communist, sensitive to the power of propaganda, and dependent 'on the leadership principle, hero-worship, quasi-spiritual inspiration, paligenetic imagery, and Romantic longings for national regeneration' (p.159). But although the BUF deployed ex-suffragettes, whose motives are perceptively probed by Gottlieb, their numbers were few. Moreover, there is always a temptation to equate suffrage militancy with the leadership style of Emmeline and Christabel Pankhurst, when in fact the Women's Social and Political Union was not simply their creation. And however useful it was for the BUF to associate itself with suffrage militancy, most feminists were opposed to fascism.

Another theme which is given a new appraisal is the sexual politics of Sir Oswald Mosley, with Gottlieb going beyond his personal relations with women to an assessment of the social significance of fascism for a limited number of elite admirers; to the contrast between Mosley's literary persona and his actual behaviour; and to the quirks of his particular brand of masculinism, which left him little time to define the new fascist woman. *Feminine Fascism* also provides a welcome assessment of the experiences of the BUF women who were interned during the Second World War and who turned genuine hardship into a claim for martyrdom, relating their incarceration to the concentration camps of Nazi Germany. The book concludes with a lengthy Who's Who in the History of Women and Fascism in Britain: something which is interesting in itself and will be of real use to future reseachers.

Overall, what emerges from Gottlieb's study is the positive attraction that fascism had for some British women, to whom it offered at least as many practical opportunities as the existing political parties, whilst stressing its ability to rise above party. Women who valued excitement, extreme nationalism, imperialism, the expression of racial pride and the spurious certainties of the extreme right, found a welcoming home in the BUF. However, there are issues on which the reader is left wanting more. It would have been useful to have a fuller account of women fascists during the 1920s, and especially of their political activities. The contributions of national women leaders still emerge more clearly than those of regional activists. And we learn more about the pronouncements on feminism and fascism by feminine fascists and feminists than about any personal contacts between the two.

Christine Bolt
University of Kent at Canterbury

Duncan Tanner, Chris Williams and Deian Hopkin (eds), *The Labour Party in Wales, 1900–2000* (Cardiff, University of Wales Press, 2000), xxi + 324pp., ISBN 0 70831 586 0, £35.00 hbk; ISBN 0 70831 719 7, £14.99 pbk.

Wales has traditionally been seen as part of the Labour heartlands. The party has held the biggest share of Welsh seats at every general election since 1923 and four party leaders have represented Welsh constituencies. Labour's supremacy in Welsh politics reached a peak in the 1960s when it dominated local government and won 32 of 36 seats at the 1966 general election. But, as this book celebrating the party's centenary demonstrates, the historical picture is more complex than such simple facts and figures first suggest.

The book is a scholarly but accessible collection of essays that combines themes with narratives in spanning the century since Keir Hardie was elected MP for Merthyr in 1900. As its important historiographical introduction sets out, the book draws together and synthesises work available elsewhere but it also contains new, original and important contributions to the study of Welsh and British politics. It also steps beyond conventional political spheres to assess the party's contribution to Wales and the Welsh people. It is not an official history and the party is not beyond criticism. What emerges from the essays is a party of dedicated and right-minded people but also one that, on occasions, suffered from 'limited horizons, timidity, defensiveness and particularly from male chauvinism' (p.16).

The first four chapters explore the period before Labour gained ascendancy in the aftermath of the First World War. John Williams succinctly but comprehensively lays out the social and economic context, whilst also pointing out that there was no straightforward link between such conditions and political change and attitudes. Deian Hopkin explores the party's pre-1900 roots, Eddie May looks at local Labour politics, while Richard Lewis concentrates on ideological issues such as religion and socialism through the Welsh language.

Duncan Tanner begins the next section by outlining the patchy inter-war growth of the party. He concentrates on the whole of Wales rather than just the southern coalfield that too often dominates writing on Welsh history. The chapter also demonstrates one of the party's recurrent weaknesses: its elitism and over reliance on a small number of influential leaders. Andrew Walling demonstrates a similar problem in the 1950s and early 1960s when weak grassroots organisation left too much power in the hands of a few leaders. In contrast, Chris Williams's chapter on inter-war local government, demonstrates what has often been one of the party's strong points: its pragmatism in adapting and responding to situations beyond its liking (such as the inter-war depression) in order to serve its communities. Kenneth Morgan's essay on war and reconstruction, 1939-51 shows that it was the 1945 general election that actually marked the beginning of Labour's real domination of Welsh politics. In the following years, as Walling notes (p.193), in parts of Wales voting Labour became 'a way of life, passed on from one generation to the next'.

The essay by Neil Evans and Dot Evans provides a detailed history of the long involvement of women in the party. It acknowledges the weakness of Labour's overall record here, but, in concentrating on what was achieved, is perhaps a little disappointing in its probing of the chauvinism that it acknowledges. There is nothing uniquely Welsh about such attitudes and this is a book on the Labour Party in Wales rather than the Welsh Labour Party. Yet, as R. Merfyn Jones and Ioan Rhys's important essay demonstrates, Labour has been more committed to devolution than is often supposed or conceded. Although always incorporating a great many dedicated unionists, Labour has also included its share of devolutionists who have played their part in pushing forward the overall cause and the hesitant debate that accompanied it. Some will disagree with the emphasis placed by the chapter on the pro-devolution sentiments of elements of the party but they need to be acknowledged alongside the fact that it was a Labour government which, albeit cautiously, delivered the National Assembly for Wales.

Like most of the chapters, Jones and Rhys's chapter emphasises the importance of individuals to the party and its policy. By acknowledging the human element of the social and political life of the party, the book steps beyond the simplistic interpretations sometimes made by political science. Thus, as the book demonstrates, there was never an automatic and unquestionable link between Labour and the working class, and local and national electoral successes often owed much to the sheer efforts and popularity of individual party workers and representatives. Furthermore, for many party workers Labour was as much a social activity as a political machine.

There are, of course, gaps in the book's coverage, particularly in the post-1945 section. The party in rural Welsh-speaking Wales gets rather short thrift throughout. Local government since the Second World War, the scene of some of Labour's most important achievements and failures in Wales, is almost completely overlooked. Yet these are reflections on the current state of research rather than the editors' oversights and the book never claims to be definitive. Instead, it sets out to identify subjects for future research. This is most apparent in Duncan Tanner's thought-provoking final chapter which reviews the last thirty years. Covering a broad spectrum of issues, it raises many questions, such as the grassroots support for New Labour, that will be central in future research on the party.

Historians of the party elsewhere will recognise from this book that there has often been little to distinguish Labour in Wales from other areas of the UK where it has enjoyed strong electoral support. Indeed, a comparative approach to the regional history of the party would be very illuminating.

Nonetheless, at the end of Labour's first century, devolution has created a new kind of Welsh politics. The results of the 1999 National Assembly elections, which saw Labour lose heartland seats such as Islwyn and Rhondda, and the 2001 general election, where it won 34 out of 40 Welsh seats, suggest that people vote differently in specifically Welsh elections. If the Labour Party wishes to dominate the Assembly in the twenty-first century in the way it often did local and central elections in the twentieth, then it must embrace a new *Welsh* agenda.

This fine book is a testimony to the party's past successes and failures. As the introduction notes (p.16), the overall record is 'more positive than negative' but Labour should not be complacent. For its own and Wales's sake, it should look to its history and see the importance of policies that are pragmatic but still ultimately guided by a desire to serve local communities. This means realising that the new Welsh politics requires a specifically Welsh approach.

Martin Johnes
Lecturer at St Martin's College, Lancaster

Jonathan Rose, *The Intellectual Life of the British Working Classes* (New Haven, Yale University Press, 2001), ix + 534pp., ISBN 0 30008 886 8, £29.95 hbk.

This is an important and genuinely original book. It sets itself a challenging task: 'to enter the minds of ordinary readers in history, to discover what they read and how they read it' (p.1). In large measure it succeeds. Throughout the emphasis is on the consumption rather than the production of culture—what Rose terms a 'history of audiences', and others might call a history of 'reception'. The principal source for this innovative project is the testimony of working-class autobiography, which Rose uses to demonstrate that working people could find inspiration and life changing meaning in the most unlikely texts. He thereby reminds us that texts are open to a multiplicity of readings, not just by post-modern critics, but also by working-class readers struggling on the road to self-education. Rose brilliantly demonstrates how literature could be appropriated to challenge supposedly 'natural' hierarchies of social and cultural power—how it became a vital resource in the project to find an independent working-class political voice in the nineteenth and early twentieth century. He also shows how it could play a vital part in more personal stories of liberation—encouraging individuals to question the inevitable and the injustice of their impoverished lives.

Of course one could perhaps quibble with the title—despite a few useful discussions of working-class life and culture *in general*, especially the chapters on school and culture, this is overwhelmingly a study of the British autodidact tradition and its shifting relationship with 'culture' and cultural elites. Moreover, its definition of 'working class' is a broad one—clerical and other office workers loom large in the study, and even teachers and manufacturers are included so long as they suffered from 'a lack of a basic education' (p.73). As such the study offers important confirmation of the common culture that could bind manual and non-manual workers in urban, industrial Britain—the culture of self-education and the mind. Rose acknowledges that autodidacts represented a minority among manual workers, but rightly insists that they were a sizeable and profoundly influential minority. In support of this claim Rose provides an interesting range of survey data suggesting that approximately one-in-four manual workers were part of this self-educated minority in the early twentieth century (pp.190, 193, 230, 235).

The book works best when the autodidact culture is clearly centre stage, but is less convincing when seeking to make generalisations about working-class culture on the basis of a critical reading of autobiographies combined with a few sketchy opinion surveys from the 1940s. Thus in the chapter on culture we get a brief discussion of popular awareness of politics and current affairs which uses a few atypical autobiographies (mostly rural) to stress that all too often 'ignorance was stunning' (pp.220-3). Doubtless it was in many families, but as an analysis of the general level of politicisation the discussion is not entirely adequate. The discussion of popular attitudes to empire (chapter 10) is more detailed, but not fully convincing. Indeed it is here that we face most starkly the basic methodological problems of Rose's study. Again, the case is woven largely from autobiographical reminiscences, which we are told were either silent about empire, or deeply sceptical (p.335). However, as Rose himself readily admits, his sample of autobiographies is, of necessity, unrepresentative of the working class as a whole—skewed, as it is, towards the most literate, and the political left-wing (p.2). This matters little when the topic for investigation is working-class literacy or attitudes towards facets of British left culture (e.g. the interesting chapters rehabilitating the WEA, or the one explaining autodidact hostility to Marxism), but when the subject is political attitudes in general it matters a great deal. Moreover, on some topics, and empire is a perfect example, the retrospectiveness of autobiography becomes a fundamental barrier to the reclamation of contemporary feelings and meanings. Not only are Rose's writers disproportionately from sections of the working class that we might assume to be sceptical about the claims of empire, but their testimonies are written in the wake of imperial decline. Moreover, Rose's claim that tales of imperial daring and adventure had little impact on working-class youth cannot easily be reconciled with his own evidence about the popularity of G. A. Henty's stories and the 1924 Wembley Empire Exhibition (pp.348-50), or his acknowledgment, in a later discussion, that such stories could capture the imagination of working-class girls (p.379).

Finally, we must explore Rose's arguments about the decline of the auto-didact tradition he outlines with such skill in *The Intellectual Life of the British Working Classes*. The spectre of decline hovers over the book from the out-set since in the preface we are told that, after the Labour landslide of 1945, 'the working-class movement for self-education swiftly declined, for a num-ber of converging reasons' (p.11). However, this story of decline is never systematically outlined, and it is, in truth, not wholly persuasive. The book ends with a clever, but ultimately overly schematic, argument about the post-war triumph of an elite-dominated 'culture industry' at the expense of inter-war 'middlebrow' culture, whose roots, we are told, had lain in the con-servative cultural traditions of the working- and lower middle-class autodidact (chapters 12 and 13). However, many of the most celebrated mid-dlebrow writers had no links to the plebeian traditions explored by Rose (one thinks of Coward, Christie, Sayers and Sheriff, for instance), while post-war high culture has continued to be permeated, and profoundly influenced, by self-conscious 'outsiders' denied the advantages of birth (here one might include Pinter, Sillitoe, Potter, Emin, and for that matter Lennon and McCartney). Again the problem lies in part with Rose's choice of sources. Rose's autobiographers display an understandable tendency to celebrate their early struggles for self-education and their selfless motivations, and to den-igrate the complacent and utilitarian view of education in the (post-war) present. However, that does not mean that when those born in the 1960s begin to write their autobiographies, some at least will not turn out to have found the same wonder and inspiration from their discovery of 'culture' as the writers whose memories shape this book. Whether there will be as many stories of *shared* exploration of the forbidden world of culture is less clear, but even here we should perhaps be wary of premature judgement. Certainly, the proliferation of informal reading groups in recent years (by no means all irredeemably bourgeois), the popularising of new literature through Booker-style jamborees, and the massive increase in the sales of 'classic' lit-erature might all be integrated into a less pessimistic assessment of British popular intellectual life at the turn of the century.

Jon Lawrence
University of Liverpool

Sue Branford and Bernardo Kucinski, *Politics Transformed: Lula and the Workers' Party in Brazil* (London, Latin America Bureau, 2003), ISBN 1 8936 561 3, £6.99 pbk.

In October 2002, Luiz Ignácio de Silva (known as 'Lula'), the ex-metal-worker leader of the Workers' Party (the Partido dos Trabalhadores, PT), was overwhelmingly elected (57 per cent) as Brazil's president. This event (perhaps the most significant Latin American election since Allende in Chile in 1970) sent shock waves throughout the continent, startling a US Administration already worried by the wave of maverick Latin American leftists coming to power.

What the victory highlighted was the remarkable achievement not just of Lula (a real 'migrant rags to presidency' story) but even more of his party, which, growing out of an eclectic mix of Catholic radicalism, Marxism, populism and the disaggregated informal sector, became, despite harassment and repeated electoral defeats, the first truly popular and national class-based party in Brazil (including in its number the eco-activist Chico Mendes and the radical educationalist Paulo Freire). That trajectory also marked a change in the party under Lula's firm charismatic leadership, sewing together the often contradictory parts into a winning coalition of the left, but without losing the support of the 'new unionism' which had spawned it in the 1970s or the Landless Movement which its partly reflects.

It is that story which this book recounts. The first in a promising new series of Short Books from a Latin America Bureau production-line famous already for pithy, readable, committed analyses, it offers a timely explanation that is all the more convincing for being written by two experienced Brazilianists, both with a past or present in journalism but both with a deep knowledge of Brazilian politics, a sharp political eye and a sense of optimistic commitment (that does occasionally tend towards the hagiographic).

That journalistic focus gives the book its strengths and its shortcomings. One clear strength is the study's immediacy (which a more deeply analytical research tome could not achieve), offering us both a wealth of informative detail and an astute account which takes us from the dark days of the illegal union struggles against the military regime, through the apparent rise and fall of a party that, after threatening in 1989 (with 44 per cent of the vote) to take Brazil by storm, then collapsed into relative division and irrelevance, overwhelmed by the modernising social democracy of Cardoso (a phenomenon which is especially well studied and explained by Branford). Yet, surprisingly but rightly, the authors choose to focus not on Lula's personality but, rather, on the nature of the PT itself, a richer source of analysis.

Inevitably, that same approach, however, necessarily omits such deeper issues as the particularities of post-1950s Brazil—and especially the economic, social and political evolution of the South-East—the crisis of the military regime after 1974, and the (highly relevant) importance of Liberation Theology. Also, perhaps not enough is made of the PT's national profile, a significant departure from previous Brazilian patterns.

However, these criticisms are not serious enough to detract from the value of this study, whose strengths make it a necessary contribution to our understanding of a remarkable phenomenon that could change our reading of Latin American politics.

Antoni Kapcia
University of Wolverhampton

David Coates (ed.), *Paving the Third Way. The Critique of Parliamentary Socialism* (London, Merlin Press, 2003) ISBN 0 85036 512 0, vi+270pp., £16.95 pbk.

Michael Newman, *Ralph Miliband and the Politics of the New Left* (London, Merlin Press, Monthly Review Press and Fernwood Publishing, 2002) ISBN 0 85036 513 9, xiv+368pp., £15.95 pbk.

Recent years have seen the marked resurgence of interest in the New Left, with a wealth of scholarly monographs, articles and group biographies flooding the academic presses and injecting fresh life into the study of an intellectual movement which, at the height of its powers, promised to comprehensively re-fashion radical politics in Britain.[1] Ralph Miliband was among the foremost of its luminaries, a brilliant and inspirational teacher, whose erudite and exacting writings provided a searing critique of the apparent failures of successive post-war Labour governments, while offering a compelling vision of the creation of a fresh Marxist grouping, based upon the organised working-class, that was capable of achieving socialism. Highly influential throughout the late 1960s, when the last 'Indian summer' of western Marxism gripped many university campuses, and again during the wave of grass-roots activism that swung the Labour Party leftwards, during the 1970s and early 1980s, his works have since either been ignored or comprehensively distorted, in order to sit more easily with the curious blend of historical amnesia, revisionism and—all too often—downright ignorance, which has hallmarked the 'New Labour' project since its inception. Writing shortly after Miliband's death, in May 1994, Tony Benn could only lament that his was a 'life [that had] passed without any comment' from the media and from his immediate political heirs, alike.[2]

In consequence, the publication of an impeccably researched biography, benefiting from access to private and professional papers, and of a compilation of his writings, and those of his closest associates, drawn from the pages of the *Socialist Register*, of which he was co-editor—alongside John Saville—from 1964 onwards, can only serve to focus the attention of a wider audience upon his rich intellectual legacy. As such, both books are to be warmly welcomed by the readership of this journal, complementing each others' strengths and establishing a coherent, and sympathetic, picture of the clarity, drive, and sheer individuality of thought that characterised Miliband's prolific oeuvre. Setting aside his early research on the popular ideology of the French Revolution, and escaping from the shadow cast by his original patron, Harold Laski, Miliband devoted himself to a thorough analysis of the limited impact made upon capitalism by social democracy, and by the British Labour Party in particular. It was his profound, and well-reasoned, belief that it was 'Labourism'—that particular preoccupation of the Labour Party with parliamentary procedure rather than with the pursuit of true radicalism—that had allowed the capitalist classes, and the state that they controlled, to consistently absorb the impact of socialism and to render the handful of dissenting left-wing MPs, who had slipped through the establishment net, as isolated figures, far removed from both the levers of true power and from the permitted 'mainstream' of political discourse. Such arguments about the very nature of the Labour Party, and the potentially disastrous course it had charted during the Cold War era, through its slavish devotion to US foreign policy, form the core of Miliband's essays chosen from the *Socialist Register*, and may yet come to assume an unexpected contemporary significance as the gap between hope for—and reality of—the present Labour government appears to be visibly widening, against a background of adventurist wars and collapsing public services. In this light, Miliband's concept of a progressive 'Third Way', thoroughly divorced from the one-nation platitudes of the mid-1990s, has the capacity to acquire a fresh relevance.

As Michael Newman makes clear, Miliband—having maintained a critical distance from the Communist Party after the late 1940s—suffered no sudden disillusionment with revolutionary Marxism, following the Hungarian rising and the revelations of Khrushchev's 'secret speech'. As a result, he appears to have been relatively free of the feelings of bitterness, regret, and betrayal that had marked many of those who formed the first New Left after 1956, and was able to chart a path towards a broad, and non-sectarian, brand of Marxism that sought to enshrine both individual and collective liberty. Wary of any attempt to import doctrines uncritically from abroad, Miliband engaged in a furious and—as Newman shows—ultimately tragic debate with Nicos Poulantzas, defending his own innovative and empirical Marxist analysis of the state against the somewhat arid structuralism of Althusser's great disciple. While frequently impatient and sometimes hot-tempered, it is Miliband's sense of decency and common humanity, whether reflected in his shock and regret over Poulantzas's suicide, or in his gritty determination to maintain his ideals in the face of an increasingly hostile political and academic climate, that emerges so forcefully throughout the biographical study. As ideological fashion changed, and many of his peers chose to abandon Marxism in favour of post-modernism, and the study of consumerism, Miliband attempted to come to terms with the profound trauma inflicted upon organised labour by the ravages of Thatcherism. Rejecting the 'New Revisionism' espoused by *Marxism Today* and many of his former colleagues among the New Left, he continued to argue that the working class was the necessary, and utterly indispensable, 'agency of historical change'.[3] It is this sense of his optimism, tenacity and principle, in the face of growing adversity, which Newman so successfully conveys in the final chapters of his pioneering work, and which together with the well chosen and lovingly reprinted extracts from Miliband's own writings, form a fitting and timely tribute to a major figure of the Left who has at last been made the subject of such incisive and, indeed, inspirational forms of study and comment.

John Callow
Goldsmiths College, University of London

Notes

1. See for example Lin Chun, *The British New Left* (Edinburgh, 1993); Michael Kenny, *The First New Left. British Intellectuals after Stalin* (London, 1995); Bryan D. Palmer, *E.P. Thompson—Objections and Oppositions* (London, 1994).
2. Tony Benn, *Free at Last. Diaries, 1991–2001*, ed. Ruth Winstone (London, 2002), p.247.
3. Newman, op.cit. p.284.